LETTERS THAT GET ACTION

C.L. Keyworth

ARCO PUBLISHING, INC.
NEW YORK

Published by Arco Publishing, Inc.
215 Park Avenue South, New York, N.Y. 10003

Library of Congress Cataloging in Publication Data

Keyworth, C. L. (Cynthia L.)
  Letters that get action.

  Includes index.
  1. Commercial correspondence. 2. English language—
Business English. I. Title.
HF5721.K46 1984   808'.066651   83-21344
ISBN 0-668-05694-0 (Reference Text)
ISBN 0-668-05700-9 (Paper Edition)

Printed in the United States of America

Contents

This book is for Lou and the fellowship.

Acknowledgments

The author wishes to thank her friends for their help during the writing of this book, especially Rhoda Clary, Cathie Early, and Wendy Salinger.

Special thanks are due to the following people, who gave assistance and shared professional information:

Bob Holland and Virginia Petersen of the Better Business Bureau of Metropolitan New York

Gary Walker, New York City Department of Consumer Affairs

Nancy Cahn, constituent services for Representative Bill Greene (R-NY)

Lisa Linden, director of constituent services for State Senator Roy Goodman (R-NY)

Ruth Shapiro, President, Ruth Shapiro Associates, New York City

1.

GETTING ORGANIZED

Organizing Work Space

Everybody needs an office. Homemakers, male and female, need a place to stash bills, letters, and papers; to write checks and answer mail; to keep correspondence and records. Teenagers need a place to study, to keep their books and school supplies and their correspondence with chums, pen pals, and the people they do business with (e.g., model boat manufacturers, suppliers of collectible stamps). The business of daily life *is* a business: it generates paper, recordkeeping, and bookkeeping, sometimes in what seems like overflow amounts.

By an office I don't mean a room of one's own. That's a luxury few of us have. But an office can be made anywhere, in the corner of a room or on an unused tabletop. Home offices can be very simple or incredibly elaborate but they have three basic elements: (1) a surface on which to work, (2) a place to keep papers, and (3) a place to store supplies. Here are my suggestions for efficiently creating—and using—these elements.

• Make an office space.

If you're lucky enough to have a desk, then that's your office. Maybe it's a desk you share with your wife or husband or your school-age children. That's a good way to maximize use; just make sure everyone has fair access and leaves everything tidy after he or she has finished working. Perhaps you have a desk you've forgotten about—your grandmother's rolltop antique in the hall or a student desk that one of your grown-up children has abandoned in the attic. If so, dust it off, tighten the knobs, oil the hinges, and use it.

1

If you can afford to buy a desk, choose one with built-in files and lots of supply space. Office furniture stores often have sales on used or damaged desks and desk chairs; metal desks in gunmetal grey are usually good buys. Although they are not beautiful, these pieces are functional and sturdy; try painting them with high-gloss spray enamel. A wonderful desk idea that has recently become popular is a door-sized piece of wood placed on two file cabinets.

Office spaces can be set up in all sorts of places, wherever you can find a surface that's big enough to work on. Try using dining surfaces when not in use: breakfast bars, kitchen tables, dining room tables. Any small table, purchased at a thrift shop or rediscovered in the garage, can be painted or stripped and placed in the family room, kitchen, sewing room, or bedroom.

• Make a place to keep papers and store supplies.

The best way to keep and organize papers is in a file system. (See the discussion on filing in the next section, "Organizing Information.") If you don't have a permanent work space, you can still find a permanent place to keep files and supplies. Try clearing out a permanent space in the linen closet or the bottom drawer of a bureau. Supplies—paper, stationery, pens—can be stored in a box on a closet shelf. Use a shoe or garment box, or buy a cardboard storage box at a variety or stationery store.

Storage space must be both safe and convenient: safe from such domestic misfortunes as spilled airplane glue, and convenient to reach, not hidden behind back issues of magazines or old photograph albums.

• Keep supplies on hand.

One of the best ways to encourage an efficient flow of correspondence is to have a good stock of supplies. It is expensive, time-wasting, and discouraging to discover at the last moment that you're out of stamps, typewriter ribbons, or stationery.

For diversity of merchandise at reasonable costs, shop at a stationery store which serves small businesses as well as the general public. Avoid boutique stationery stores that sell greeting cards and gift items; they're usually more expensive and don't offer enough choices. If you shop at variety stores or supermarkets, you can sometimes find good buys in the school supplies section. Scout sales and discount stores. Add to your office inventory once or twice a year.

Basic Office Inventory

Paper. For business letters, use white typing paper, 8½ × 11 inches. If you buy bond paper, a good choice is medium weight (16 lbs.) which has enough heft to fold and handle easily but isn't as thick as parchment. However, this is a matter of personal taste. My favorite paper, for both personal and professional use, is photocopy paper; this is available at copy centers in packages of 500 sheets for about $5.00. It is of decent quality and considerably cheaper than most typing paper stingily packaged in 50-sheet boxes and sold in stationery stores. Do *not* use onionskin paper or paper which may be erased because they are too easily smudged. Do *not* use paper in any other color than variations of white (ivory, cream, light grey) or paper with decorations or illustrations.

For personal letters, of course, you can use any paper you want to, including yellow-lined school pads, scratch paper, or the backs of your children's (or your own) drawings.

Personal stationery. Choose it with an eye to its restraint and good taste. Subdued colors—beige, blue, ivory—and minimal decorations are less distracting. And there's no reason why women's stationery should be decked with flowers or why men's stationery should sprout bird dogs and ducks. Choose a classic design, a neutral color, or a plaid envelope lining, and you and your mate can use the same paper. If you choose paper printed with your name and address or a monogram, let the printing be simple and unobtrusive.

Scratch paper. You can buy ready-made note pads or you can make your own by cutting up used paper and stapling it, clean side up, to a piece of cardboard. For drafts, notes to yourself, grocery lists, etc., buy yellow-lined paper or inexpensive "second" sheets.

Pens and pencils.

Paper clips, rubber bands, transparent tape, letter opener, scissors, ruler.

Stamps. Buy rolls of 100 and avoid waiting in post office lines every week. Keep stamps of assorted value in stock for sending heavier letters and packages.

Home postage scale.   This is a real time-saver. Scales come in all sizes for all purposes; a scale that weighs up to two pounds and costs around $12 to $15 will probably suit your needs. You can get a free copy of current postage rates from the post office.

National Zip Code Directory.   Available at your local post office.

Address book or Rolodex.

Calculator.

Wall calendar.

Appointment calendar.

Staples, stapler, staple remover.

Typewriter.   Whether you consider this a luxury item or not depends on your job, the amount of writing you regularly do, the presence of students in your home, and the kind of letters you write. But for many people, the typewriter is indispensable.

It is, unquestionably, a useful piece of equipment. It is essential for producing job application letters and businesslike consumer and citizen action letters. It comes in handy if you bring home work from the office or school; it is helpful for producing term papers, book reports, readable directions, and recipes. And many people nowadays type personal correspondence. This is an acceptable practice—in fact, typing is preferable to half-legible handwriting.

If you buy a typewriter, choose one with convenient features like an automatic return and a self-correcting device or correcting cartridges. Choose a clear, easy-to-read typeface; do not use a script face for business letters. Always use black ribbons for business writing.

Typewriter correction fluid and correction paper.

Files and file folders.   (See the next section, "Organizing Information.")

Desk chair.   Swivel chairs with adjustable height and back angles can be found at office furniture stores. They aren't cheap, but they're worth it if you do a lot of writing. They improve posture, reduce lower backache, and even ease eye strain by putting you into the proper relationship with your desk. (Sit at your desk the way secretaries are taught to do: knees pulled under the desk and back straight. Don't sit a foot away from your desk and hunch forward to reach it.)

Lighting.   Good, inexpensive lighting can be found in office supply stores, houseware departments, and variety stores. Clamp-on lamps with flexible arms can be attached to your table or desk and focused on your work area. They are available in many bright colors, usually for under $20.

Adequate lighting is not a luxury; it's a necessity for the health and comfort of your eyes. Bad lighting makes an hour's worth of bill-paying or letter-writing more tiresome than it need be.

Storage units.   For paper, carbon paper, scratch pads, even files, one of the best choices are the sturdy plastic stackable trays available at stationery stores. They're also available in metal, usually in "office colors" like gunmetal green, black, or grey. They fit on desk tops or on shelves. For small items like paper clips, rubber bands, and erasers, you can buy small plastic units with two or three little drawers and a place to hold pens and pencils. Large coffee mugs are also useful for this purpose, as well as for holding scissors and rulers.

Wall-hanging storage units.   These are made especially for papers; you can also use new or used shoe bags or kitchen storage units. Tape category names on each pocket: *Utilities, Bills, Automobile Expenses, Letters to Be Answered,* and so forth. This is a useful item because it acts as a visual reminder of things to do and bills to be paid.

Bulletin board.   Think of a bulletin board as a file folder on display. It is for all those items such as *Things to Do, People to See,* and *Appointments to Keep.* It can also act as a non-file—for the things you haven't yet organized.

Bookcases or bookends.

Organizing Information

Every household, like a business, has a flow of information coming into it and a flow going out. The in-flow includes: bills, notifications of services and sales, records (e.g., bank statements), personal mail, printed material like magazines and newspapers, announcements of upcoming events, invitations, charitable and commercial appeals for your money, and miscellaneous things (e.g., Aunt Betty's recipe for graham cracker ice cream). Out-flow includes: payments, personal mail, orders, and so forth. The best—really, the only way—to handle this flow of information (i.e., paper) is with a filing system.

• File everything.

I used to think that the motto "A place for everything and everything in its place" was only for the super-organized, those men and women who have order in their fingertips. But they probably have natural file cabinets in their heads. It's the mildly disorganized (like me) for whom files are a blessing.

In general, a filing system can be defined as any procedure which maintains information according to selected categories. Informal filing systems include separate piles of mail on a desk top, separate cubbyholes in an old desk, or even drawers in a bureau. The basic fact about filing systems is that they tend to attract order; once there's "a place for everything," it's an easy step to putting everything in its place. And with the categories in existence, you can find what you need.

If you want a special and safe place for your file folders, get a file cabinet to house them. One- or two-drawer metal file cabinets can be gotten at fairly reasonable prices at discount or used office supply stores. Even cheaper are cardboard file holders, available at stationery or variety stores. If you can find a box in which the files can stand upright, use that. You might spray it with colorful enamel paint to make it more cheerful and professional-looking. You can also, in a pinch, put file folders in drawers or filing trays. In that case, you won't be able to read the labels easily so you might try color-coding the files with stick-on labels: red for bills, blue for personal mail, and so forth.

Files can be organized according to any convenient principle. You can simply alphabetize them according to the first letter on the file label. Another useful, and common, approach is to place files in descending order of their importance or use to you. Here are some common file categories:

Bank statements and savings books
Investments
Rent or mortgage payments (includes tax-deductible expenses related to house or apartment)

Utilities bills and records
Telephone bills and records
Charge card statements
Current taxes (includes unearned income, sources of revenue
    other than wages, records of deductable expenses, etc.)
Legal documents (includes birth certificates, passports, mar-
    riage license, wills, deeds to property, keys to a safety de-
    posit box, sales contracts and warranties)
Tax statements and returns for the past five years
Personal correspondence (with copies of your responses)

• Create resource files.

You may have plenty of pieces of paper floating around which
do not fit into the businesslike categories mentioned here. You can
preserve this information as a resource file in categories like these
which people have found useful:

Movie reviews (current ones clipped from newspapers and
    magazines)
Restaurant reviews (ditto)
Flyers for local businesses
Charitable appeals (that may someday be answered)
Articles on consumer goods

• Make your own consumer guide.

It's useful to have a separate address book or Rolodex of businesses you patronize regularly or think you may someday use.
Along with the name and address of the firm, also jot down information about the goods and services available there. Here is one
such entry:

The ABC Cheese Shop
123 Wabash Avenue
Hudson, NY 12534
Telephone: (914) 555-7279
Hours: 9–6; Sundays 12–6.

Excellent cheddar and English stilton; also fresh cream cheese
without preservatives. Brie always on sale at $3.95 a wheel. Herb

teas and gift items at low prices. Millie Hobson's son Jerry is the
manager; he's the one who dropped out of State U. to take cooking
lessons.

- ● **Create your own reference library.**

Every home office needs a basic reference library for checking
spellings, locating the right word, fact-finding, and research.

Basic Reference Library

For a basic reference library, choose one dictionary, one usage
manual, and one fact source.

1. Dictionaries

The American Heritage Dictionary of the English Language
Funk & Wagnalls Standard College Dictionary
The Random House Dictionary of the English Language
Webster's Seventh New Collegiate Dictionary (This is the shorter
   version of *Webster's Third.*)
Webster's Third New International Dictionary

2. Usage Manuals

Bergen Evans and Cornelia Evans, *A Dictionary of Contemporary
   American Usage.*
H. W. Fowler, *A Dictionary of Modern English Usage.*
William Strunk, Jr. and E. B. White, *The Elements of Style.*
   (This is a sensible and beautifully written little book; highly
   recommended.)

3. Fact Sources

Information Please Almanac, Atlas and Yearbook, (New edition
   every year)
The World Almanac and Books of Facts (New edition every year)

Expanded Reference Library

4. Atlases

Goode's World Atlas
Hammond Medallion World Atlas
National Geographic Atlas of the World

5. Quotation Sources

Bartlett's Familiar Quotations
Oxford Dictionary of Quotations

6. Synonym Finders

Roget's Thesaurus (The alphabetized version is easiest to use.)
Webster's New Dictionary of Synonyms

7. One-Volume Encyclopedia

The New Columbia Encyclopedia

Organizing Time

Deal with correspondence promptly!

What good, firm advice! But how to follow it? The people who answer their mail promptly don't know the joys and terrors of pro-crastination. They don't know what it's like to have a file labeled "To be answered" which includes a 1955 Christmas card. They don't know what it's like to put off bill-paying until some weary midnight, only to realize you've run out of checks. They live in a prompt and confident universe in which there are no delays of their own making.

For the rest of us, time is an accordion which expands and con-tracts according to whim. If we don't have punctuality in our hearts, then we have to do a little external organizing. Here are some suggestions:

• Set office hours.

In setting aside one or two times a month to pay bills and answer letters, choose a time when you'll be rested and in good spirits. Saturday morning is a good choice; you then can feel virtuous about spending the day in more active pursuits. Or pick a time when you can reward yourself with a treat afterwards—say, in the early evening before an old movie on television you've been wanting to see. Or do it on your lunch hour when the shortness of time will force you into efficiency. In fact, setting time limits is a good idea; it keeps you focused and prevents you from dawdling.

Life wouldn't be lively if it were a set of regulations and rules. So, if you can't meet your own office hours, be flexible and work another day. But clearing a monthly time and space for paperwork does give you a sense of continuity and accomplishment. It gives you the encouraging sense that these sometimes dreary tasks can be done painlessly—and well.

• Be prepared.

Treat your work space and time in a businesslike way. Clear your work surface of all distractions (the latest newsmagazine, for example). Collect the necessary supplies before you sit down; have at hand: sharpened pencils, pens that work, a decent ribbon in the typewriter, and sufficient paper. A dictionary should be within easy reach. (There's no better formula for procrastinating, as any writer will tell you, then collecting supplies piecemeal during the course of a project.)

• Handle each piece of paper only once.

This little rule is almost revolutionary in its simplicity. Successful businessmen and businesswomen have been using it for years.

Consider how most people deal with a piece of incoming mail. They get a bill, a statement, or a notification of a sale, for example. They open the envelope, idly flip through the separate pieces of paper (usually two or three, although there may be as many as a dozen), but *they don't really read the contents*. At best, they may focus on one item of information—the amount due, for example—which they then forget. Then they stuff everything back in the envelope and put it away. A little later, perhaps that day or the next, they sit down to "really" read the communication; by this they mean repeating the original process, shuffling through the pieces of paper, and dawdling over the items of information. But they still take no action.

Finally, when they get around to what they consider an appropriate time—and it may be weeks later—they repeat the process a third time, this time paying the bill or ordering a sale item.

You can see what a waste of time this is. And it tends to reinforce the association many people have between inefficiency and paperwork.

Here's a better way to do it:

When you handle the mail, make three piles: (1) personal correspondence, (2) bills, and (3) everything else.

Read your personal mail at your leisure; file it right after you read it.

File bills in a properly marked file folder *without opening*. There's no need to open most bills; there should be no big surprises in your electricity, telephone, even credit card bills. If you get an "occasional" bill—say, from the doctor or dentist—then of course you should open it to check the amount and due date. Otherwise, file without opening and open your bills file during the one or two times each month you've set aside for that purpose.

With "everything else," you have three choices and you should—since you're only going to handle each communication once—only make the decision once. Your choices are:

1. *Throw it out*. Remember, the wastebasket is a legitimate— and efficient—file cabinet. You can reduce paper flow at the source by asking yourself: "Can I live without this?" If your answer is "yes," then chuck it.
2. *Display it*. If you receive dated material—a flyer from the local little theater or a sale notice—then tack it up on a roomy bulletin board with the important dates circled in red. Stick the bulletin board anywhere—kitchen, hallway, television room. Keep it current by checking it regularly and by removing "deceased" material once a week and once a month.

3. *Put it in a "Someday File."* This is a file for people who can't
make decisions, who are addicted to saving things, or who
always say "Someday I may need this!" Label this file
"Someday" or "Miscellany" and forget it. One rainy afternoon a year, go through it and weed out what's no
longer interesting. The virtue of the "Someday File" is
that you don't have to think about it—you just fill it.
Probably, if you were really energetic, you could subdi-
vide it further—for example, you could make a file on
"local restaurants that deliver" or "sales." But life is short.

• Write your answer on the letter received.

Businesspeople are making this a common practice; secretaries
often leave a space for a response at the bottom of a letter or
memo. Of course, it doesn't work for personal letters, which you
probably want to keep, but it's an excellent time-saver when answering brief notes, requests for information, etc. If you're answering a business letter, you don't have to retype the name, title,
and address, and you don't have to hunt around for appropriate
letter paper. (It was provided by the sender.)

The chief advantage of this procedure, however, is psychologi-
cal. It simplifies the task. It reduces the fuss. It eliminates the preparation, elaborate or otherwise, and gets you into the heart of the
action.

If you need a record of the original letter and your response, take
the document to the copy center on the way to the post office.

• Be inventive in the letter forms you choose.

Think of new ways to answer letters that make the job easier and
save you time. For example:

1. Tape-record messages.
2. Write memos instead of letters. Memos allow you to be
   informal, and you can be as brief or as long-winded as you
   like.
3. Send large-sized postcards. A postcard lets you put down
   one or two important thoughts or questions. It eliminates

the need for introductions and chitchat. And you don't
need an envelope.

4. Have different size paper for different length messages.
   You can use note paper, postcards, note cards (3 × 5,
   5 × 7), memo cards, wide-lined school paper, or greeting
   cards. Postcards and greeting cards now come in a variety
   of sophisticated patterns and art reproductions which can
   be found in museum shops, gift and specialty stores.

Here's how one man handles some of his extracurricular mail.
He uses regular 5 × 7 note cards, typing the name and address on
the plain side and the message, memo-fashion, on the lined side.

```
              SUBJECT:  Class of '65 Reunion

To:      "Shorty" Shortcake

From:    John Hancock

Date:    February 2, 19--

Shorty, I'm sorry to hear responses to our reunion

invitation have been poor.  Some suggestions:

    ● Scratch the beer bust and toga party

    ● Substitute informal seminar on Mid East politics

      with one of the younger professors

    ● Integrate wives into all activities (The stag

      lunch is a poor idea!)

    ● Make the Dean's speech -- "Liberal Arts:  Quo Vadis?"

      optional.
```

• Be inventive in how you answer personal mail.

The best advice good letter writers give is this: Write about what
you're doing *right now*. In other words, you don't have to write a
history of yourself and your family for the last six months. You can
focus on your present activities, passions, work, and preoccupa-
tions. What did you do this weekend? Last night? Today? What

you write about doesn't have to be significant or important. Your friends just want to hear, as it were, the sound of your voice.

Writing about the past gives your letter the flavor of leftovers. Save the histories for the end of the letter; then give a brief review of jobs, illnesses, events, etc. Writing about the *now* gives your letters freshness and immediacy.

Focus on the small, the specific, and the descriptive. You went on a picnic: What did you eat? What flowers were blooming? What birds did you see? You ate an ice cream cone: What flavor?

Describe your emotions or the mood of an event. You went to your son's high school graduation: How did you feel, besides proud? Was the mood of the day exciting, exhausting, disappointing, joyous? How did Uncle Joe feel about it all? (Ask him!)

If you don't have much to say, send something: a recipe, a newspaper clipping, a photograph, a child's drawing, your drawing (even if you can't draw, you can sketch a child's face or a cat's sprawl), a pressed leaf from the backyard maple, a quotation, a question, even one line.

PS: It's never too late to write a letter. A friend of mine sat down the other day and wrote an old family friend whom she hadn't seen for years. Her Auntie Fay, as she called her, wrote back right away with love and gratitude (no recriminations, no "why haven't you written?") *It's never too late to connect.*

Suggested Reading

Scott, Dru. *How to Put More Time in Your Life.* Rawson-Wade Publishers, Inc., 1980.

Winston, Stephanie. *Getting Organized.* W. W. Norton & Company, Inc., 1978.

2.

BUSINESS LETTER MECHANICS

The Correct Form of a Business Letter

There are many ways to arrange a business letter on the page, depending on the placement of heading and signature and the indentation of paragraphs. Here are two common and popular letter forms.

Block Letter Style

All material in this form is typed flush left. It is easy to remember, easy to type, and it looks self-contained and elegant.

Please note the basic parts of a business letter in the Block Letter Style example on page 16.

Indented Letter Style

The first line of each paragraph is indented five to seven spaces; the heading, closing, and signature are placed to the right of the body of the letter. Because of the paragraph indentation, this form looks more like printed material.

You will find an example of Indented Letter Style on page 17.

BLOCK LETTER STYLE

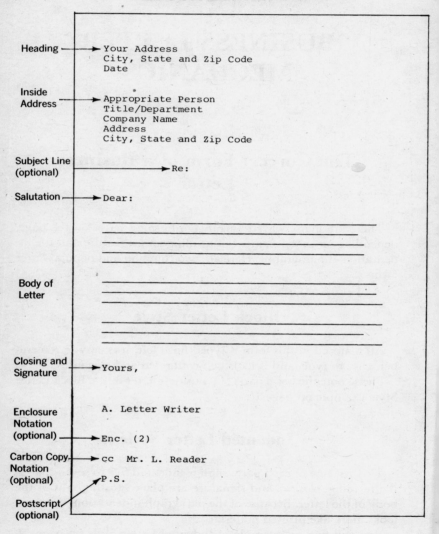

Heading ——▶ Your Address
City, State and Zip Code
Date

Inside
Address ——▶ Appropriate Person
Title/Department
Company Name
Address
City, State and Zip Code

Subject Line
(optional) ——————————▶ Re:

Salutation ——▶ Dear:

Body of
Letter

Closing and
Signature ——▶ Yours,

A. Letter Writer

Enclosure
Notation
(optional) ——————▶ Enc. (2)

Carbon Copy
Notation ——▶ cc Mr. L. Reader
(optional) ——▶ P.S.

Postscript
(optional)

INDENTED LETTER STYLE

```
                              Your Address
                              City, State and Zip Code
                              Date


Appropriate Person
Title/Department
Company Name
Address
City, State and Zip Code
Dear:

        _____
     _____
     _____

        _____
     _____
     _____
     _____

        _____
     _____



                              Yours,


                              A. Letter Writer

Enc.

cc  Mr. L. Reader
```

Memorandum Style

The memorandum style is usually used in interoffice or interorganizational communications, but it can also be adapted for regular letter use. The memo has an efficient, businesslike quality and has the advantage of grouping together certain pertinent information (addressee, sender, subject, date).

The memo is typed flush left; the enclosure and copy notations follow the text as they do in the letter. You may initial your designation or sign your name after it, or you may sign your name at the end of the memo.

```
To:       Consumer Relations Department
          The Fly-by-Night Fishing Rod Co.
          123 Wabash Avenue
          Anytown, U.S.A.  12345

From:     Mary Jackson
          1000 St. Marks Place
          New York, N.Y.  10003
          (212) 555-4340

Re:       Rainbow Rod Model #54433

Date:     September 15, 19--
```

```
Enc.
     Order form (photocopy)
```

Components of the Business Letter

Heading

Spell out the name of your state if it is one word; for two words, you may abbreviate: N.C., N.Y., etc. If the second line of the heading is long, place the state and zip code on one line together. Spell out months, and use one of the following forms for writing the date:

> May 19, 1984
> 19 May 1984

Inside Address

Make sure, first of all, that you have the proper spelling of both the name of the person and the company you're writing to. Make a last-minute phone call to the company, if necessary. (This is particularly important if you're applying for a job.) Include both the individual's title and his or her department, if they're known. The length of the line determines where you place the title.

> Mr. William Smith-Thompson
> Vice-President, Consumer Affairs
> The Successful Business, Inc.

> Mr. W. W. Smith
> Vice-President
> Consumer Affairs
> Socko Socks, Inc.

In choosing a courtesy, honorific, or professional title, always be guided by the way the individual identifies himself or herself, if known. For example, some holders of doctoral degrees or those with specific academic status choose not to use the honorific.

In addressing women, use the individual's choice:

> Miss Dorothy Reeves
> Mrs. Dorothy Keyworth

Mrs. Robert A. Keyworth
Ms. D. Keyworth

If marital status is unknown, use *Ms.* or omit the title. Omission of the title is becoming more popular today for both men and women. This permits the letter writer to be consistent in the treatment of titles, since the titles for women are so often unknown.

Subject Line

The subject line tells the reader at a glance what the letter is about. Also, it functions as a kind of title for the letter, under which all future correspondence can be grouped. It's useful for some business and consumer letters, but its brisk, memo-like style is inappropriate for job application letters.

Type the subject line: (1) flush left (consistent with block letter style), (2) centered on the page, or (3) following the indentation of the letter. Usually the subject of the letter is expressed in a phrase, not a complete sentence. You may type it in all capital letters or underline it if you wish.

The subject may be preceded by the introductory terms "Subject" or "Re." If no preceding term is used, it might be a good idea to capitalize or underline the subject to set it apart from the rest of the letter.

Subject: April inventory reports
Re: Billing error
Subject: My defective Widget Model #123
My defective Widget Model #123

Salutation

Type the salutation one double-space below the inside address. Capitalize only the first word of the salutation and the proper name, with one exception: To Whom It May Concern. Here are some examples of inside addresses with their corresponding salutations:

- **Mr. W. W. Smith**
  Vice-President
  Consumer Affairs
  Socko Socks, Inc.

  Dear Mr. Smith:

- **Geraldine Bratte**
  President
  Bratte Lawn Equipment

  Dear Geraldine Bratte:
              or
  Dear Ms. Bratte:

- **The Elite Racquet Club**
  (organization, all men)

  Gentlemen:

- **The Ladies Literary League**
  (organization, all women)

  Ladies:

- **Secretary**
  The Elite Racquet Club

  Dear Sir:

- **The Saturday Bridge Club**

  Gentlemen and Ladies:

- **Centreville Gas & Light**

  To Whom It May Concern:

Body of the Letter

Center the letter horizontally on the page. Margins should be uniform on all sides and be between one and two inches wide. Make sure you've left plenty of white space to make the letter readable. For very short letters, you may double-space or use 1½-space spacing, if your typewriter has it.

If you choose to indent for paragraphs, indent five to seven spaces. Keep paragraphs short. Double-space between paragraphs, regardless of whether you choose block or indented style.

Try to keep your letter to one page. If there's a second page, it must have at least two lines of typing on it. Avoid "widows" on the second page—widows are short, single lines, shorter than the width of the letter body. Do not hyphenate the last word on the first page.

Type the second page on plain paper the same kind as the first. Leave a top margin of at least an inch. You may, if you wish, type an identifying line on the second and succeeding pages; this line derives from the name of the company or person you are addressing:

> Bratte Lawn Equipment   p. 2   June 20, 19—
> *or*
> Bratte Lawn Equipment
> p. 2
> June 20, 19—

Double-space between the identifying line and the first line of text on page 2.

Closing and Signature

The closing you choose is very much a matter of personal style. Capitalize only the first word of the closing:

> Very truly yours,
> Truly yours,
> Cordially yours,
> Sincerely yours,
> Sincerely,
> Yours,
> Best wishes,
> Best,

Most people have a variety of handwriting styles, depending on their mood and varying between a somewhat tight, formal style and a hurried scrawl. You ought to have a signature for formal correspondence which falls somewhere between the two—bold but neat, in other words. Leave five spaces between the closing and the typewritten signature, more if you write large. Your typewritten signature must appear exactly as you wish to be known. However, your handwritten signature can differ from that or be less formal.

Jane Mack

Mrs. Robert Mack

Joseph Clemson

Dr. Joseph Clemson

Elsa

Professor Elsa Wright

Enclosure Notation

An enclosure notation refers the reader to the fact that you have included other pieces of paper with the letter. Type the enclosure notation flush left and center it vertically on the space remaining in the letter, preferably at least four spaces below the signature. For safety's sake, you may wish to identify the documents you are enclosing.

```
Enc.
Enclosure
Enclosures
Enclosures 3
Enclosures (3)
Enclosures
    Invoice #98765
    Check #56789 (photocopy)
Enclosures: 1. Invoice #98765
            2. Check #56789 (photocopy)
```

Copy Notation

The copy notation, cc, stands for carbon copy, although it may, of course, be a photocopy or other reproduction. Use this notation if you wish to signify that you are sending copies to other persons or organizations. It is typed flush left below the signature or the enclosure notation.

cc   Mr. Howard Greene

cc   The Better Business Bureau
        The Centreville Gazette

Postscript

The postscript may be used deliberately to: (1) provide emphasis or (2) lend an informal moment to an otherwise formal letter. It should not be used as a repository for significant information which should have gone into the main body of the text. The postscript may be handwritten.

PS. Give my best to Joanne and her sister.

P.S. Remember, the due date is Friday.

PS: Thanks again for showing me the communications system.

Envelopes

The envelope should be the same color and quality as the letter paper. Type the envelope neatly and professionally, although it will probably be discarded when the letter is received and filed. Nevertheless, the envelope is part of the impression you make, and some bosses open their own mail.

Suggestions for folding 8½ × 11 paper and inserting in envelope:

Small business envelopes.   Fold the sheet in half from the bottom, leaving a narrow margin at the top. Then fold in thirds, starting from the left, leaving another narrow margin at the right.

Large business envelopes (regular "letter" size).   Fold in thirds, starting at the bottom. For the second and final sheets, fold down and leave a narrow margin at the bottom.

Mailing the Letter:
Some Guidelines

The United States Postal Service uses electronic equipment to "read" envelopes. Following U.S.P.S. guidelines gets your letter to its destination with more speed and safety.

- Eliminate punctuation, including punctuation in names.
- Capitalize everything in the address.
- Use abbreviations suggested in the *National Zip Code Directory.*
- Zip code should appear on the last line of both the mailing and return address, following city and state. Allow a maximum of two spaces and a minimum of one space between the state abbreviation and the zip code.
- When mail is addressed to multi-occupancy buildings, include all room or suite information. U.S.P.S. reminds us: *Any address should be complete to the point of delivery.*
- In cases where both a post office box number and a street address are used, mail will be delivered to the address appearing on the line next to the bottom.

		GRAND PRODUCTS INC
		100 MAJOR STREET
Mail will be	────	PO BOX 200
delivered here		PORTLAND OR 97207

		GRAND PRODUCTS INC
		PO BOX 200
Mail will be	───→	100 MAJOR STREET
delivered here		PORTLAND OR 97213

- Single-space the mailing address. Keep margins of at least an inch on the right and left sides, but no more than three

inches from the bottom. Single-space the return address.
- Type mailing notations such as FIRST CLASS below the stamp.
- Type address notations such as PERSONAL or PLEASE FORWARD a triple-space below the return address.

Some Examples of Envelope Style

Conventional Style

Miss Margaret Fuller
76 Yankee Folly Road
Arlington, Virginia 22204

Mr. and Mrs. Kips Bay
25 MacDougal Alley, Apt. 6
New York, New York 10004

Mr. Terence Plautus
c/o The Author's Guild, Inc.
234 W. 44th Street
New York, New York 10021

Mr. J. Walter Reeves
Lost Hollow Farm
R.F.D. 1
Fairmont, Virginia 22130

U.S.P.S. Style

MISS MARGARET FULLER
76 YANKEE FOLLY ROAD
ARLINGTON VA 22204

MR AND MRS KIPS BAY
25 MACDOUGAL ALLEY APT 6
NEW YORK NEW YORK 10004

MR TERENCE PLAUTUS
C/O THE AUTHORS GUILD INC
234 W 44TH STREET
NEW YORK NEW YORK 10021

MR J WALTER REEVES
LOST HOLLOW FARM
RFD 1
FAIRMONT VA 22130

U.S.P.S. Two-Letter Abbreviations for States

Alabama	AL	Idaho	ID
Alaska	AK	Illinois	IL
Arizona	AZ	Indiana	IN
Arkansas	AR	Iowa	IA
California	CA	Kansas	KS
Colorado	CO	Kentucky	KY
Connecticut	CT	Louisiana	LA
Delaware	DE	Maine	ME
District of Columbia	DC	Maryland	MD
Florida	FL	Massachusetts	MA
Georgia	GA	Michigan	MI
Hawaii	HI	Minnesota	MN

Mississippi	MS	Pennsylvania	PA
Missouri	MO	Puerto Rico	PR
Montana	MT	Rhode Island	RI
Nebraska	NE	South Carolina	SC
Nevada	NV	South Dakota	SD
New Hampshire	NH	Tennessee	TN
New Jersey	NJ	Texas	TX
New Mexico	NM	Utah	UT
New York	NY	Vermont	VT
North Carolina	NC	Virginia	VA
North Dakota	ND	Washington	WA
Ohio	OH	West Virginia	WV
Oklahoma	OK	Wisconsin	WI
Oregon	OR	Wyoming	WY

3.

WRITING CLEARLY

Writing Well

Several years ago, when Washington, D.C.'s Union Station was being renovated, a decision was made to tear up the floor of the big, central hall. A hole was excavated and in the hole was installed step seating and a slideshow with sound. The slideshow lasted twenty-two minutes and consisted of snapshots of Americans at play. Making a pit in the floor of the classically beautiful Union Station was bound to be controversial. Perhaps for this reason the slideshow was not called a slideshow. The people who designed it called it instead a "Primary Audio-Visual Experience."

The purpose of language like this is to divert us from the facts. We are meant to think something is better or grander than it is. *Item: One slideshow* doesn't look very grand; better call it something else before you ask the taxpayers to pay for it. But snapshots are snapshots; even the smallest child won't think they are a "primary experience."

High-blown language is a favorite device of politicians, bureaucrats, and advertisers. Such language is also chosen by specialists like social scientists, educators, and technocrats. Knowledge of special language confers special status. Legal language is a good example of specialized communication which confounds rather than communicates:

All acts done by my agent pursuant to the powers herein during any period of disability or incompetence or uncertainty as to whether I am dead or alive have the same effect and enure to the benefit of and bind me and my heirs, devisees and Personal Representatives as if I were alive and competent and not disabled.

You can see that one of the characteristics of this language, in addition to having a special vocabulary (pursuant, enure, devisees), is wordiness. More words must mean more impressive communication, based on the theory that we're impressed by what we can't understand! Here are some further examples of wordy writing by specialists:

> There are five cost factors worthy of comment which amplify our view that home health care offers a major opportunity for older people and for our country.

> One of the very important factors to be emphasized if we think of leadership training for the children in the gifted population is— how to train them to use their skills in almost all situations?

Now, if experts write like this (and get paid for it!), should we do it too? Wouldn't we be taken more seriously if we used more words? How can we express important ideas without big important-sounding sentences?

The answers to these questions are: No, no, and easily.

Writing well means writing concisely and naturally; by doing this, we can certainly outshine the expert who is in love with his own words. We will, in fact, be taken more seriously if we write lean prose and are easily understood.

In business writing—the kind you use in writing effective letters—it's the ideas, not the words, that should get noticed. With this in mind, I've revised the sentences quoted previously. I think you'll agree they are more readable with their wordy undergrowth pruned.

> If I'm disabled, incompetent, or if it's not known whether I'm dead or alive, then my agent has the power to act on my behalf. His acts have the legal effect of being my acts, and they are binding.

> Home health care for older people costs less for five reasons.

> How can gifted children be trained in leadership so that they can use their skills as much as possible?

Business writing is speaking in print. It doesn't require a different set of mental muscles or attitudes. The reader doesn't want high-toned stuff; he needs information. Satisfy that need and chances are you'll be most persuasive.

• Forget style.

Style is a delicate matter—and an often overused word. People with a certain kind of self-confidence or flair are said to have style. When newspapers wanted to upgrade their women's pages, they started calling them "style" sections. Style is something we are encouraged to acquire.

When a writer sits down to write, his thoughts often leap to the finished product—the typed letter or printed piece. He thinks that his language had better be stylish or creative; it had better dazzle; it must impress. Naturally, this seems like a big job, and the writer becomes self-conscious. His writing, instead of being stylish, seems stilted and forced.

The best way to create style in writing is to stop worrying about it and concentrate on your subject matter. In other words, focus on *what* you're saying, not *how* you're saying it.

• Trim the fat.

Dozens of words might refer to wordiness in writing: puffy, swollen, bloated, lumpish, packed, crammed, stuffed, inflated, overgrown. Don't you itch to free your writing from the fattening effect of too many words? Don't you want to be a master of economy in prose?

To do so, develop an eye for the unnecessary in writing. In the old days, printers used pieces of metal, called lead, to space out a line of type. Some writers use words like printer's lead to fill up a sentence. If you do this without thinking, ask yourself: Which words contribute to the meaning of the sentence and which are merely fillers? Which words make the sentence go and which seem dead and useless?

Wordy	**Revised**
There was unanimity about the choice of Paul Smith for the position of secretary.	Everyone agreed Paul Smith should be secretary.

Wordy	**Revised**
I am particularly desirous of becoming associated with an institution such as yours.	I'd like to work for you.
I would prefer to find again a situation where I would be assigned the challenge and responsibility of regional sales representative.	I'd like to keep working as a regional sales representative.
Whereas the Widget has virtually stopped functioning, it has ceased to be an effective piece of machinery.	The Widget doesn't work.
Enclosed please find my resume, which indicates the full range of my skills and capabilities.	Here is my resume.
I'm looking forward to meeting with you and discussing our problems to our mutual advantage.	Let's talk.
If I can be of any further assistance, please do not hesitate to contact me.	Let me know if I can do anything else.
Pursuant to our telephone conversation of this morning, I return herewith my Widget which no longer functions.	Here is my defective Widget.
Is it possible to meet with you at your earliest convenience concerning the matter of the new position in the accounting department?	May we talk soon about the new job in accounting?

Not This	**But This**
In the event that	If
In the case of	If
Consequently	So
As a consequence	So
Due to the fact that	Because

Not This	**But This**
For the reason that	Because
Despite the fact	Although
Concerning the matter of	About
She has been persuaded	She believes
She is of the opinion	She thinks
With the result that	So that
Regardless of the fact that	Although
Made contact with	Called, wrote, saw
It is often the case that	Often
Is the recipient of	Received, got
With regards to, in regard to, as regards	On, about
With respect to, respecting	On, about
In the absence of	Without
According to him	He says
In addition to	Besides, also

• Begin at the beginning.

Dogs turn around a few times before they lie down. Batters take practice swings before they face the pitcher. Public speakers begin their remarks with a long string of greetings: "Mr. Smith, Mrs. Smith, distinguished guests, ladies and gentlemen. . . ." None of us would dream of asking for a favor until we had made small talk: "How's the wife? the kids? How's Rover?"

Many of life's actions appear to require preparation and introduction. Communications, we think, require a preface. We dislike just beginning; it seems too abrupt. So part of our impulse toward wordiness stems from our dislike of beginning at the beginning. We hem and haw before a speech. We write long introductions where none are necessary, and we pad our sentences with unnecesssary opening phrases.

But when there's an important piece of information to be communicated quickly, we give it efficiently. If we can't make a business meeting, for example, we get right to the point. We are direct and straightforward when there's urgent information to be communicated.

Business letters are, in fact, pieces of urgent information. Since they are generally impersonal, extended forms of politeness are unnecessary. In addition, incidental information about your life, the

Unnecessary Openings

THE ABC WIDGET COMPANY
77 Price Street
Centerville, Ohio 45459

Dear Sirs:

I am seventy years old and today my
bursitis is kicking up so bad I can
scarcely hold a pen. I've been trying
to write this letter for weeks, but
I'm so mad I could spit. Now, bursitis
or no bursitis, I'm going to get this
off my chest.

Begin here ➤ I bought a Widget last year and it
doesn't work. . .

Acme Accounting Office
123 Main Street
Centerville, Ohio 45459

Dear John Smith:

My wife and I moved to Centerville a year
ago and have loved the place ever since.
We've made many friends here, and of
course we know my wife's cousin, Harold
Tintern, who was with the Fire Department
for forty years. We intend to settle here
for good. With that in mind, I thought
I'd write you.

Begin here ➤ As a professional accountant with fifteen
years' experience. . .

state of your emotions or your health, the history of how you came to write the letter—all these are irrelevant. Don't waste your reader's time with them. Begin with facts, with some persuasive piece of evidence, or at the beginning of your story: "On July 4, I bought my Widget" or "I'm applying for the position of book-keeper." The sample letters on page 33 show examples of unnecessary openings.

- **Omit unnecessary opening phrases.**

Not This	**But This**
I have ascertained that Widgets are sold for $19.95 in other area stores.	Widgets are sold for $19.95 in other area stores.
It is my belief that a good secretary needs more than typing and shorthand.	A good secretary needs more than typing and shorthand.
It is interesting to note that the sale of home computers has risen dramatically in the past two years.	The sale of home computers has risen dramatically in the past two years.
Let me point out my strong skills as a salesman.	I have strong skills as a salesman.
In the event of a change of plans, I will call you.	If I change my plans, I will call you.
Let me add that I am disappointed in my Widget.	I am disappointed in my Widget.
It is suggested that you read the business magazines regularly.	Read the business magazines regularly.
It has been shown that job-sharing reduces absenteeism.	Job-sharing reduces absenteeism.

Note: Often, the introductory phrases "there is" and "there are" can be left out.

Not This

There are many men in my department who worked hard preparing the report.

There is a popular notion which has it that women are better talkers than men.

But This

Many men in my department worked hard preparing the report.

A popular notion has it that women are better talkers than men.

- ## Don't be redundant.

A student raises her hand and begins speaking with an apology: "This is only my personal opinion." What other kind of opinion could she offer? An impersonal one? Somebody else's? Of course not, but *personal* gets stuck like a burr to a lot of other words: personal interview, personal relationship, personal physician. It isn't incorrect to use *personal* in this way; it's just repetitive, or redundant.

Redundancy comes from a Latin word meaning "to overflow." It means excessive, unnecessary, and wordy. Some redundancies occur so often that we scarcely notice them, or use them without thinking. But their use weakens our writing.

Redundant

The model I bought has four speeds and is *green in color*.

The reason why I am dissatisfied with my Widget is *because* it is the wrong size.

I would like to set forth the *true facts* of the case.

I've been working in *close proximity* with our advertising department.

I can *prove conclusively* that my car is a "lemon."

I was in charge *throughout the entire* project.

Revised

The model I bought has four speeds and is green.

I am dissatisfied with my Widget because it is the wrong size.

I would like to set forth the facts of the case.

I've been working closely with our advertising department.

I can prove that my car is a "lemon."

I remained in charge of the project.

Redundant	**Revised**
There was *consensus of opinion* among the experts.	There was a consensus among the experts.
The *end product* was a revised handbook.	The product was a revised handbook.
Last week I saw the *same identical* mower for $20 less.	Last week I saw the identical mower for $20 less.
The instructions were not *clearly legible*.	The instructions were not clear. (were not legible)
I received no *financial remuneration* for this work.	I received no pay for this work.
	or
	I volunteered for this work.
It's *obviously clear* that morale is up in my department because of my elimination of *useless waste*.	It's clear that morale is up in my department because I've eliminated waste.
The *unfortunate mishap* occurred yesterday morning.	The mishap occurred yesterday morning.
During this *course of time*, the car broke down twice.	During this time, the car broke down twice.

- ## Choose short words over long ones.

A three-syllable word, some writers think, is superior to a one-syllable one. The reason is that longer words are often derived from Latin or Romance langauge words and have an airy sense of learning about them. The short words are often our homegrown Anglo-Saxon ones; they are thought too down-to-earth to be impressive. On the contrary, longer words often look self-conscious and forced.

Of course, not all synonyms mean exactly the same thing: you don't want to say *love* when you mean *infatuation*, for example. But when two words mean nearly the same thing, choose the shorter one.

Long Words	**Shorter Synonyms**
delinquent	late
enlargement	growth
expire	die

Long Words	**Shorter Synonyms**
facility	ease
acquiesce	consent
comprehend	know
inquire	ask
inhabit	live in
expeditious	speedy *or* prompt
vehicle	car, bus, truck
sufficient	enough
attempt	try
articulate	say
initial	first
depart	go
implement	do
acquire	get
supplement	add to
utilize	use
individual	man, woman, person
beverage	drink
consume	eat
domicile	house
prevaricate	lie
remuneration	pay
transpire	happen
cooperation	help
demonstrate	show
expenditure	cost *or* expense
initiate	start *or* begin
purchase	buy
relate	tell
remittance	cash
remit	pay
accomplish	do
require	need
affirmative	yes
approximate	about

- **Use the active voice.**

Passive

The hiring guidelines were written by me.
The final decision was made by me.

Active

I wrote the hiring guidelines.
I made the final decision.

As you can see, using the active voice places the emphasis on the actor—in these cases it's "I"—rather than on the thing acted upon. Using the active voice generally produces stronger, crisper sentences.

Passive Voice	**Active Voice**
Important changes were produced by me during the first year.	I produced important changes during the first year.
A new safety record was established by me for my department.	I established a new safety record for my department.
The school board was persuaded to adopt curriculum changes.	I persuaded the school board to adopt curriculum changes.
In addition, the annual fund-raising dinner dance was coordinated by me.	In addition, I coordinated the annual fund-raising dinner dance.
For three years, the company newsletter was written and edited by me.	I wrote and edited the company newsletter for three years.
The division was instructed in the use of the new machinery.	I instructed the division in the use of the new machinery.
A guide to the most recent tax exemptions was put together by me.	I put together a guide to the most recent tax exemptions.

- **Connect ideas.**

There are many rules for good writing, but one is almost guaranteed to upgrade even the most awkward writing. Like all good rules, it is not a gimmick, but is based on clear thinking. Here is the rule: *Make the relationship between sentences explicit.* Let's see how it works.

I increased sales by 51%. I was promoted to regional sales manager.

What's the relationship between the increased sales and the promotion? If the promotion is the result of the writer's sales achievement, then that relationship should be made explicit:

> I increased sales by 51%. *Therefore,* I was promoted to regional sales manager.

Instead of "therefore," the writer could have used "as a result" or "so" or any of several words or phrases. The point is that in the revised version, the relationship between the sentences is explicit. *Explicit* comes from a Latin word meaning to unfold or spread out—in other words, to make plain to the reader. Using transition words like "therefore" helps the writer clearly connect ideas from one sentence to the next, making the relationship plain.

You can use transitional words and phrases to do the following:

Amplify what you've said

And, moreover, further, furthermore, in addition, besides, too, also

Make comparisons and contrasts

Likewise, similarly, but, yet, however, nevertheless, still, on the other hand, in contrast

Enumerate

First, second, next, in the first place, first of all, finally, last

Express time

To begin, at first, soon, then, meanwhile, afterward, last

Make examples

For example, for instance, to illustrate

Intensify a point

Indeed, of course, clearly, in fact

Reach conclusions

Therefore, so, thus, as a result, as a consequence, consequently, naturally

Summarize

In other words, to sum up, in brief, in short, to summarize, in conclusion

Weak	Revised
I was at the factory at the appointed time. It was closed.	I was at the factory at the appointed time. *But* it was closed.
My new Widget broke down three weeks after I bought it. My old Supreme lasted ten years without a repair.	My new Widget broke down three weeks after I bought it. *In contrast,* my old Supreme lasted ten years without a repair.
I replaced time clocks with time sheets. Staff morale was greatly improved; late arrivals were reduced.	I replaced time clocks with time sheets. *As a result,* staff morale was greatly improved; *for example,* late arrivals were reduced.

Sometimes transition words are used when emphasis is desired.

Weak	Revised
The economy is in a recession and unemployment is on the rise.	The economy is in a recession and unemployment, moreover, is on the rise.
I was head of my department for five years and served as liaison officer with the president's office.	I was head of my department for five years. In addition, I served as liaison officer with the president's office.

• Forget paragraph rules.

Most of us were taught in English classes that the paragraph is the basic unit of composition. The paragraph is defined as a group of sentences (usually a minimum of three) developing a central idea; this central idea is clearly stated in a topic sentence. These are good rules for nonfiction composition, but they aren't useful for letter-writing.

First of all, because letters are usually short, they are not suited to presenting ideas in a leisurely fashion. In a letter, many different ideas and facts may be presented within one paragraph. (Using transition words will insure that these different ideas are clearly connected.)

Second, besides organizing ideas, the paragraph's function is to break up chunks of prose, to make information look readable. Letter writers can take advantage of this and produce short paragraphs. Short paragraphs look inviting, and they make your information more accessible. You may vary paragraph length and structure in any of the following ways:

- Write paragraphs of only one sentence.
- Write a series of very short paragraphs or alternate shorter with longer paragraphs.
- List a series of items in a series of paragraphs.

Take a tip from printed material and lay out the letter in any way to make it appealing, interesting, or more readable. You may:

- Use dashes, asterisks, or bullets to itemize information. (Bullets are formed on the typewriter by typing a lower-case "o" and filling it in with ink.)
- Underline important material.
- Group material under headings or subheadings.
- Use indentation and spacing freely.

Here are some examples of unconventional paragraphing and layout.

WHAT'S WRONG WITH MY ACME WASHER MODEL 115

1. The washer stops on the rinse cycle about 30 percent of the time.
2. White clothes washed in the washer look dingy.
3. The spin cycle leaves clothes still dripping.
4. During the spin cycle, the washer makes a loud noise and moves six inches to the side.

WHAT I WANT DONE ABOUT MY ACME WASHER
1. I want the washer removed by your delivery truck no later than Thursday, February 17.
2. I want a full refund of my purchase price, based on the conditions of my "money-back guarantee" listed in the contract.

As service representative for North American Claims, I accomplished the following:

• Established computer-sharing with the head office.
• Created flexible work schedules for field representatives.
• Assembled a selling kit for new representatives.

• Revise, revise.

Two associates meet for a business lunch. The subject is lowered efficiency in the accounting department. The language is simple and to the point. The tone of the conversation is practical, cordial, and at times, humorous and personal. But when one of these associates sits down to write a business letter or memo on this subject, her common sense seems to desert her. She slips into pompous language, overwriting, jargon words. Since she is writing, not speaking, she changes her style from conversational to Late Business English—very unreadable. Here is her memo:

```
Date:    December 1, 19--
To:      John Jones
From:    Mary O'Day
Re:      Lowered efficiency in the accounting department


         It is my impression that the reasons for lowered

efficiency can be traced to many causes.  I'd like to

propose some questions, which, while not readily answerable,

may help shed some light on the problem.  In the absence of

factual data, I can only make some surmises.  Has there

been an increment in absenteeism, both in the form of late

arrival for work and in sick leave?  Could functional

skills levels be improved?  Could existing skills be
```

utilized to improve productivity? Is software
state-of-the-art? Could advancements in computer science
be accessed to improve efficiency? What personnel would
be willing to interface on computer technology? Does the
staff lack the means to articulate professional needs and
concerns? Is the salary level of the department head
competitive laterally? Will we get sufficient cooperation
from other departments concerning this matter? I look
forward to meeting with you at the end of the week.

How would you revise this memo to make it readable? Here's
one possible revision:


```
Date:    December 1, 19--
To:      John Jones
From:    Mary O'Day
Re:      Lowered efficiency in the accounting department
```

John, without hard data, I don't have too many
answers. But I do have some questions which might be
helpful.

Is the accounting staff often late for work?
Are they getting sick more often? Are their skills
up-to-date? Could the skills they have be used better?
Do they need better machines? Would computers help?
Who in the company knows most about computers? Would he
or she help out? Can the staff talk about their problems?
Do they and the department head get paid enough? Will
we get help (for example, feedback) about this from other
departments?

Let's talk on Thursday or Friday.

Professional writers know that most writing is rewriting. If you feel awkward or unsure of your writing, then revision is essential. Think of it as an opportunity to make your writing better—tighter, leaner, more informative. You've got a first draft on paper; now try to look at your work objectively. Objectivity isn't difficult if you agree to be your own best critic. Try to take a positive pleasure in the basic job of revising, which is cutting out what's unnecessary. If you've ever gone on a diet or weeded a garden, you know it can be fun to trim the excess. In this case, it's words you have to trim—extra words, long words, wordy constructions, and redundancies.

With practice, you'll be able to edit as you write. But revision will always be an essential part of the process.

Note: For *Suggested Reading,* see the end of the next chapter.

4.

POWERS OF PERSUASION

A business letter is a kind of persuasion. It attempts to persuade the reader to take an action. Sometimes the letter asks for an immediate and definite action: Send a check! Write me back! Don't delay! Other times the desired action is more subtle—perhaps the reader won't do anything yet, but will be persuaded to keep an open mind. This is often the case with a job application letter or a memo to an associate. That's the sort of letter that says: Think about this and then get back to me.

Whatever its type, a persuasive letter forms an alliance of agreement between the writer and the reader. It creates a climate of good will in which business can take place.

An old salesman once said to a younger salesman, "Try to appear sincere!" That's impossible, since by definition sincerity must be genuine. But life isn't perfect. Sometimes we feel cranky but must be polite or are angry and must be cool. Therefore, the rule of thumb is: The ideal tone of a letter should convey the ideal tone of a letter writer. That tone should be good-natured, confident, practical, and professional.

Tone is the environment of the letter, its feel. And no matter what your own emotions are, the letter should be courteous. In real life, courtesy opens doors—literally and figuratively. In business, courtesy is the language of all transactions. In business writing, courtesy means being considerate of the reader.

• Satisfy the reader's need to know.

All communication is a contract between the writer and the reader. The writer agrees to share a piece of news, a story, an idea,

45

or information. The reader agrees to take some time to listen. By the act of reading, he says: "I want to know. Tell me."

For example, let's say you pick up an article about the history of the Brooklyn Bridge. You've never read anything about the bridge before, but now you have a reader's need to know. You expect the writer to give you facts and details, interesting information, and specifics. If he fails to do that, he fails his part of the bargain. He fails to be considerate of the reader.

A writer sometimes puts blocks in his own way by imagining the reader as a judge who's quick to deal out criticism. This is because we all have a critic inside us, and it's easy to imagine that the reader shares our inner critic's judgments.

I suggest imagining a different kind of reader, one who is sympathetic and open-minded. This reader is interested in what you have to say—he has a need to know. I can offer an immediate example of this technique. During the writing of this book, I wasn't thinking of the editors, copy editors, and publisher who would be my first readers and critics. As a matter of fact, I thought of them very little, and instead concentrated on you holding this book in your hands right now. Writing directly for you—with your strong need to improve your writing—helped me focus my own writing and keep it practical.

• Don't try to second-guess the reader.

In a great deal of professional writing, the writer must know his reader's tastes, age, income bracket, even reading level. Then he must shape his material with those facts in mind. But with the type of letters discussed in this book, it is rarely necessary to do this. Sometimes we won't even know whom we're writing to—that's the case with consumer action letters, for example.

You don't have to know your reader's sex, age, race, or size to satisfy his need to know. Here's a good example of what *not* to do, from a book on business letter writing:

> Letters to women may well stress an emotional appeal by discussing a product's beauty, attractive design, or modern styling. Letters to men are usually made more effective by a reasoned appeal stressing utility, efficiency, and economy, or the details of construction and materials.

I'll ignore the writer's assumption that women respond to emotional appeals rather than commonsense approaches. But with a large percentage of American women working outside the home, it's a safe bet that they also have a need to know about utility, efficiency, and economy. Of course, many writers will go on making appeals to readers on emotional or manipulative grounds. But good writers know that all readers have a need to know.

• Let the facts speak for themselves.

One of the best letter writers I know is a woman who works as a fund-raiser for a large nonprofit organization. She likes and respects the institution she works for, and she knows everything there is to know about it. She's got the facts at her fingertips, if they're not filed in her head. She knows the smallest details of all her institution's programs as well as such things as annual postage costs or the janitor's salary (after all, financial accountability is part of her job). When she sits down to write a fund-raising letter, she keeps in mind her favorite motto: Facts persuade.

Facts carry an authority of their own. For example, consider the following:

Sears, Roebuck & Co. is the largest retailer in this country.

In 1981, the administration proposed budget cuts which reduced energy conservation programs by 86%.

Ft. Myers is one of the fastest growing communities in the U.S., having nearly doubled its population between 1970 and 1980.

The French novelist Georges Simenon has written 150 books under his own name and another 350 under various pen names.

If we let facts speak for themselves, they will capture the reader's attention. But in order to let the facts speak for themselves, you must know the facts. This seems simple enough, doesn't it? And yet it's easy advice to ignore. *You* know your apartment hasn't had proper heat all winter. *You* know your new car is a lemon. *You* know you revamped the personnel department last year and deserve a raise. But what do you mean by "all winter"? What, exactly, is the service record of your automobile? What, precisely, were the effects of your changes in the personnel department?

• Be specific.

Readers are understandably wary of generalizations, which are often called "sweeping" because they tend to sweep things together, ignoring important distinctions. They leave a lot of unanswered questions in their wake.

Generalizations are okay for starters: "Widgets are wonderful" or "My division is very productive." But then they must be backed up with examples. Tell your reader who and what, when and where, how and why. Be accurate. Be specific.

Widgets are wonderful because they have ten speeds, five attachments, use less energy than any comparable model, and are owned by over one-quarter of all the households in America.

My division is very productive. Productivity is up 20% over last year, worker error is down 10%, and accidents are down 15%.

• Point to solutions.

Almost everyone welcomes the chance to be agreeable. Most people who work are helping out other people by providing goods, services, or information; people are in the business of saying yes. Give your reader a chance to say yes by spelling out specific solutions to problems. A problem, in this sense, doesn't have to be negative. A problem is any tangle of people, places, or things that needs to be untangled. A problem is a question that needs answering.

The letters discussed in this book present a problem, a case, or an opinion, and they ask that an action be taken on the basis of that presentation. They are useful because they point to specific actions—a vote, a political consideration, a job offered, a consumer wrong made right.

Sometimes solutions are negotiable. When this is true, you should make it clear that you're willing to make the terms adjustable. Other times, there is only one acceptable solution—a new Widget, a specific job title. When this is true, make your position clear without appearing stubborn or arrogant.

Emphasizing solutions, not problems, recognizes that the writer and the reader often have goals which aren't so different from each other. For example, the job seeker makes her case by showing how she can help a company prosper. The consumer assumes a common interest with the seller: it's in eveyone's best interests if the marketplace functions well and productively.

- ## Use positive words and expressions.

A positive tone in your letter encourages positive results. Emphasizing solutions is one way to be positive; another is to use positive language.

Not This	But This
No, I can't. No, I won't. I don't know how.	Yes, I'll try.
Never.	Perhaps. Sometimes.
I can't believe that a company I've been doing business with for nearly twenty years can't come up with anything better.	I feel sure that you'll find a quicker solution to this problem. After all, we share twenty years of business dealings and mutal regard.
Through bad timing I couldn't make it to the state convention this year.	I read about the state convention in the association newsletter and was interested to discover. . . .
You'll never get our vote again unless you can come up with some pretty fast answers.	Our continued support depends on your frank and thoughtful answers to our questions.

- ## Don't make extravagant claims.

Writers often make the mistake of overstating their case. They do so by making extravagant claims and by ignoring opposing views. A student, for example, who is writing a brief composition entitled "The Joys of Swimming" plunges into her subject as a diver plunges into the deep end of the pool. She puts down other sports and claims unmodified success for swimming. The key here is unmodified. Yes, swimming has all the advantages of other aerobic sports; it's good for the heart and produces better muscle tone and flexibility. Many people find it toning and relaxing. But the student who claims absolute success, for everyone, everywhere, and speaks of this success as if a mermaid were turning out advertising copy, has overstated her case. And for her conclusion, she states: Everyone should swim! (Desert-dwellers are urged to build pools!)

If you let the facts speak for themselves you will not need extravagant statements. These statements are almost always generalizations and contain such phrases as "the best," "the worst," "the most important," "without a doubt the single most. . . ." If you have sold more washers than anybody else in your region, you don't need to claim: "I am the greatest salesman at Acme!" If you have shown that your Widget was in the repair shop 25 percent of the first year of ownership, you don't need to state: "This is the worst product made in America!"

People tend to be suspicious of absolutes, partly because they belong to the language of advertising. You undercut your evidence and devalue your reader's common sense when you use them. Stick to facts; they are better evidence in support of action.

Suggested Reading

Bernstein, Theodore M. *Do's, Don'ts, and Maybes of English Usage.* Quadrangle, 1977.

Flesch, Hugo. *The ABC of Style.* Harper & Row, Publishers, Inc., 1964.

Flesch, Hugo. *The Art of Readable Writing.* Macmillan Publishing Company, Inc., 1962.

Hall, Donald. *Writing Well.* Little, Brown and Company, 1973.

Mack, Karin, and Eric Skjei. *Overcoming Writing Blocks.* J. P. Tarcher, Inc., 1979.

Newman, Edwin. *Strictly Speaking.* Warner Books, Inc., 1975.

Strunk, William, Jr., and E. B. White. *The Elements of Style.* Macmillan Publishing Company, Inc., 1972.

Zinsser, William. *On Writing Well.* Harper & Row, Publishers, Inc., 1980.

5.

CONSUMER ACTION

When Consumers Complain

The toaster alternates between burnt and underdone. The coffeepot cracks. Your orange juice tastes like a day without sunshine. The taxi driver leaves you at a meat processing plant on the south side of town (it wasn't your destination). Your doctor keeps you waiting for two hours, but on another occasion threatens to bill you when you can't keep an appointment. The man who cuts your hair starts chatting about his mortgage and leaves you looking like Joan of Arc. Speaking of mortgages, the bank won't give you one because of an ancient credit dispute. You can't use your credit cards because your ex-husband overcharged your account. Your department store is billing you for a sweater which began unraveling while still in the store wrapper.

Meanwhile, your travel agent books you on a tour of the Greek Islands with a busload of Albanian bureaucrats; accommodations are early pioneer. Your luggage is in Tierra del Fuego. . . . When the movers move you from Akron to Dayton, the television set arrives busted, some of the silver is missing, and there's a sizable hole in the portrait Aunt Maude painted of Grandmother.

Appliances don't work. Repairmen snarl. Deliveries aren't made. Every year hundreds of thousands of consumers buy goods or services which cheat them of their money's worth. Here, in a more orderly fashion, are some of the most familiar sources of complaints:

Breakdowns
Shoddy workmanship

Inefficient design
Poor service
High prices
Expensive maintenance
Slow or no delivery
Scanty or absent directions for use
Unsafe or unhealthy products
Failure to meet the warranty
Fine print or hidden clauses in the warranty
Failure to meet acceptable product standards
Deceptive or fraudulent advertising
Unresponsive complaint handling

With billions of buyers putting out billions of purchasing dollars each year, it's a wonder that more people aren't crying, like the vocal majority in the movie "Network," "I'm mad as hell and I'm not going to take it anymore!" But there are real obstacles to the process of expressing legitimate complaints.

First of all, the consumer is reluctant to admit he's been had. This is especially true if the consumer didn't have enough information about the product, if he made a hasty or impulse purchase, or if the product was not very expensive or was on sale. In these cases he may feel, a little uneasily, that he's got no one but himself to blame.

The seller is certainly going to reinforce those feelings. Didn't you read the tag? The fine print? Didn't you know the sale was final? Didn't you see the stain, the wobbly leg, the scratch? What do you expect for $29.95?

Secondly, the consumer isn't sure about the legitimacy of his complaint. This can be true whether he's got problems with a $10 toaster or a $300 typewriter. Does he have a major problem on his hands, or just something he should live with, maybe tinker with himself? For example, the new typewriter has a faint but high-pitched hum. It's giving him a headache. But maybe all electric typewriters hum this way. Or how about the new detergent, which cost 19¢ more than its nearest competitor. The ad on television said it would leave clothes "whiter than white." That's a serious claim! But, in fact, the sheets look rather less than snowy . . . dingy, in fact. Maybe it's the washing machine, which also has problems.

In short, a consumer may have a subjective impression that something isn't working well, but he doesn't know how to translate that impression into a persuasive argument for redress. He's not sure if his expectations are too high or are realistic. And even if the facts are clear—the car door fell off, for example—the consumer isn't sure what his rights are or what the seller is obligated to do for him.

Meanwhile, to make matters more complicated, the problem itself may change. The toaster starts working better for a few days. The car develops a new knock but loses a previous rattle. A couple of minor problems get swallowed up in a major one—what's a knock or a rattle compared to the now malfunctioning transmission? And the consumer isn't certain of the sequence of events, didn't keep a written record of complaint transactions, doesn't know the name of the salesman who offered him a genial, but verbal only, "guarantee." And where's the bill of sale anyway?

Finally, the cost of complaining can be high—in terms of money, time, telephone calls, mailing costs, research time, and emotional energy. And when the consumer does summon the will to make a complaint, he may meet with resistance from the seller in a number of ways:

- The seller can pass the buck from one employee to another within the company. Each new employee that hears the complaint is clearly unhappy or uncertain about having to deal with it. This in turn makes the consumer encourage the buck-passing process, since he hopes to end up with a knowledgeable, sympathetic listener.
- The seller can simply do nothing. This is very effective since the seller has the ability to absorb complaints the way a stone wall absorbs the beating of tiny fists.
- The seller can accuse the consumer of wrongdoing or over-reacting. The seller may say that the consumer misused or abused the product; that he didn't read the directions; that he didn't read the contract or the warranty; that he is misinformed; that he is expecting too much.
- The seller can offer apologies instead of action. If the seller's apologetic concern really seems thick, the consumer may stop making a fuss. Sometimes the seller will sooth-

ingly offer a partial action—he'll fix something instead of
replacing it; he'll give back part of the purchase price; or
he'll suggest a cosmetic change instead of restitution.

Complaint vs. Action

One of the obstacles to taking consumer action may lie in the
phrase "consumer complaint." To complain is to express dissatis-
faction, annoyance, or grievances without necessarily doing anything about them. In fact, the word complain comes from a Latin
word meaning to beat your breast—a form of expression that hurts
no one but yourself. It's not surprising that companies used to call
their consumer relations departments "complaints" departments
as a subtle form of discouragement. A complainer is a whiner
without rights.

But a revolution has been going on in consumer awareness. Consumers have been demanding better goods, better services, fair
business practices, and fair advertising. They have a right to do so,
and a responsibility. Our system only works if it works—that is, if
it is responsive to the needs and rights of the consumer.

When a consumer fails to make a problem known, he forces
other consumers to absorb continuing problems. When business,
government, or the buying public don't know about a problem, it
won't get fixed. By taking action, the consumer adds to a valuable
storehouse of information about the way goods are manufactured
and services are delivered. This information helps government regulate and improve business.

It also helps businesses themselves improve the quality of their
goods and services. Since profit is an industry's means of survival,
quality control may be lower down on its list of priorities. Consumer advocacy makes quality control a necessity, not an option
(after all, compensating buyers costs both time and money).

The purpose of consumer action is neither therapy nor revenge.
It isn't merely to ventilate your emotions or make a retaliatory
strike. Going public with a problem and getting what you deserve
(i.e., what you paid for) helps everyone.

Self-Defense in the Marketplace

There are many strategies for successful consumerism. But the best defense a consumer can have is knowledge—knowledge of the product, knowledge of consumer rights, and knowledge of the complaint process. Knowledge gives you the clout to overcome the difficulties of complaining and the resistance of sellers to your demands. Here are a series of suggestions to give you that clout, beginning with the subject of advertising, the most powerful selling tool of the twentieth century.

• Be skeptical about advertising.

Madison Avenue knows the secret of manipulating words and images. An automobile is magically associated with the prowess of a wild cat. A face cream is magically associated with the good looks of a movie star. Advertising sells its products by offering seductive promises of youth, beauty, health, money, ease, romance, better life-style, even time. There's no logical connection between a car and a cougar, but the image is powerful and presented with sophistication. We buy it and we may well buy the product.

When it comes to advertising, let the buyer beware. There are several less-than-candid techniques which advertisers use to get our attention. A product may be filmed or photographed in such a way to make it appear bigger, better, or more luscious. A product may be presented as being "unique," "one-of-a-kind," or "supreme," when in fact it's identical to other products on the market. A product may claim to be "new" or "improved" when only an insignificant change has been made. Finally, an advertiser may offer distorted truths or even tell outright lies. It takes a while for the government or the competition to catch up with false claims in advertising. Meanwhile, the public has been led to believe that a mouthwash can cure the common cold, or that bee pollen retards aging in human skin.

It's hard to avoid or ignore advertising when it constantly reaches out at us from television screens, newspapers and magazines, billboards, and store windows. Airplanes write the names of beers against the summer sky. We wake up in the morning with the tunes of cola ads jingling in our heads. If ads are not always persuasive, they are, at least, pervasive.

The consumer's best defense is awareness. He can listen to, but not learn, the emotional message broadcast by the ad. He can distinguish between what the ad pretends to offer and what it is really selling. A face cream, for example, can only do so much. It can reduce dryness and provide temporary smoothness and moisture to the skin. But it is made in a factory, not in a magician's study. It cannot turn back the clock.

• Research before you buy.

The first stop is your local library for back and current issues of *Consumer Reports*, a monthly magazine which offers comparative ratings of products. The ratings are made by Consumers Union which tests products in its own laboratories and designs appropriate standards of judgment. The standards themselves are helpful because they tell you what criteria to use when buying a product. For example, if you're thinking of buying a car, your guide may be the appearance of the car, gas consumption, and cost. But you should also be prepared to judge its maneuverability, comfort, traction and directional stability, maintenance and repair costs, braking ability, climate-control system, and so forth.

Consumer Reports comes out every month and reports on such diverse subjects as household appliances, pet foods, and cold remedies. Each December, the magazine publishes the Buying Guide which condenses the previous year's reports into a convenient paperback edition, available at bookstores (or free with a subscription). Both the magazine and the Buying Guide accept no advertising.

It's sometimes helpful, especially when considering smaller purchases, to ask friends, neighbors, and co-workers about the product. Have they discovered any real differences between detergents? Does the new low-calorie mayonnaise taste good? Is a certain brand of shoes comfortable? Does the corner dry cleaner do reliable work? One of the best pieces of consumer advice I ever got was from the check-out person in my local supermarket. As I was standing in front of an array of expensive cleaning products, she came by and tapped the house brand of ammonia for 40¢.

• Shop around.

Do your homework, get your facts in hand, then take some time and comparison shop. Don't shop when you're rushed or tired, or at the last minute. Compare prices, warranties, ease of purchase, and fringe benefits such as free delivery or installation. You can often use the telephone for the early stages of comparison shopping. Prepare a short list of questions before you call, and don't let a harried salesperson try to brush off answering you. If a company is listed in the Yellow Pages, it should be prepared to deal graciously and fully with your telephone questions.

• Become a steady customer.

Deal with companies you know, or ones that friends, relatives, or colleagues have had good relations with. Keep going to a firm whose goods or services have pleased you in the past; in this way you establish a continuing business relationship. It pays to get on a name basis with owners, managers, and salespeople. Introduce yourself to the manager of your local grocery store, to the owners of your stationery store, dry cleaner, shoe repair shop, camera store, to the salespeople at your corner boutique. Steady customers get better service, and when a problem develops, their complaints tend to get prompter and more gracious attention.

• Deal with reliable firms.

If you're making a major purchase, try to check out the firm beforehand. One good way to do this is to call the Better Business Bureau in your hometown.

The BBB serves to encourage fair dealing in the business community and to protect and inform the consumer. The BBB analyzes the validity of advertising claims and handles complaints (this service is discussed later in this chapter), but it will also give you help before you make a purchase. The BBB has files on many businesses in your area. It can give you a quick profile of a firm: how long it's been around, whether there have been complaints made against it, the kind of complaints, and the way they were handled. The BBB will *not* give you a rating of companies, products, or services, or tell you which ones are best to use.

- ## Deal with licensed firms.

Categories of firms which are licensed vary from state to state, so check with your state agencies, consumer affairs office, or attorney general's office. Companies are more likely to listen and act on consumer complaints if their license can be suspended or revoked for noncompliance with regulations.

And licensed firms, while not guaranteed to be honest by the conferral of a license, are at least apt to be more established.

- ## Deal with firms that do repairs.

It's a lot easier to bring a toaster back to your neighborhood merchant than shipping it to the manufacturer or carting it to a service center.

- ## Check warranties and contracts.

Read carefully all printed material that sets forth the terms of agreement between you and the seller. If you're handed an undecipherable warranty to sign, ask to go over it paragraph by paragraph with a manager or officer of the company. Two good questions to ask: How does this warranty protect me? What does it leave out?

Be sure everything is in the warranty before you sign it. All financial terms should be spelled out, as well as all data concerning the goods or services (model number, date of delivery, etc.). Be sure you understand the exact dollar amounts of the financial terms: minimum amount due, down payment, annual interest rate, service charges, late payment penalties, and so forth.

Keep one copy of the signed warranty and make another copy to keep in a separate file for safety's sake. Treat the warranty with the seriousness it deserves; it is a legal document.

- ## Get it in writing.

Don't accept verbal agreements. If a mechanic says he'll service that brake lining he's about to put in, have him put it in writing. As Sam Goldwyn once quipped, "An oral agreement isn't worth the paper it's written on." Right, Sam. Some less-than-honest salespeople are masters of the suggestion and well-dropped hint. In their mouths, hot air sounds like promises: the plywood is solid maple, the dicer-slicer-chopper does everything but baby-sit, and the used car you're considering was made in heaven by angels and driven by somebody with a fear of high speeds. These guys are quick to dismiss questions and doubts and to reinforce what you hope to hear with a hasty "sure" and "of course."

Listen carefully to what sounds like fast talk. Don't be intimidated into silence: Ask questions, and if you don't get answers, go somewhere else. If you're offered a tasty deal, get it on paper.

• Be aware of the "implied warranty."

The Implied Warranty of Merchantability is a section of the Uniform Commercial Code, a federal law which protects consumers against the limitations of manufacturer's warranties. The section states that every product offered for sale has to be suitable for its intended use. In other words, it has to do what it's supposed to do in order to be "merchantable" or saleable.

If you buy merchandise which doesn't live up to its intended use, and the seller doesn't correct the problem, you may revoke acceptance of the merchandise and ask for your money back. Your success with this strategy will depend on your state laws and on the amount of resistance by the seller.

• Keep careful records.

Keep all proofs-of-purchase. It's a good idea to have a file called "Purchases" that you can simply stuff with sales slips and receipts. If the sales slip doesn't say what item was bought, write that in yourself. By the way, check all sales slips at the time of purchase to see that they are both correct and legible.

• Create a written history of product use.

If you make a major purchase—an automobile, a boat, a kitchen appliance, or a piece of technological equipment—make a record from the day you start to use it. Record any failure to function, to live up to the warranty, or to fulfill reasonable expectations—in short, any time the product is more of a hassle than a help. Be specific about dates and times. Even seemingly unimportant problems can turn major or become chronic.

Keep all service and repair records. And, if you're forced to begin a complaint process, keep a record of all communications between yourself and the seller, or any other agency you deal with. This means you must keep copies of all correspondence exchanged and record the substance of telephone conversations. This is important because you may start out a complaint process in the hopes of solving it amicably. If you don't get satisfaction, these phone calls form part of the picture of the way your complaint was handled.

Effective Complaining

• Make sure your complaint is legitimate.

Have you used the product properly, following directions for performance, maintenance, and safety? Have you used the product appropriately—for example, you haven't tried to make your blender slice when it can only dice? Have you observed special usage suggestions and ways to clean and store the product? If you've misused the product in any way, it will weaken or invalidate your complaint.

• Organize your facts.

Collect all documents: receipts, billing notices, credit card bills, instructions for use (sometimes found on tags or in garments), warranties, etc. Note the date and place of purchase. Identify merchandise by color, model number, name, and cost. Jot down exactly what's wrong with the merchandise.

• Decide what action you want taken.

First, be specific. If you think that the problem is with the individual product you've purchased, then you'll probably ask for a repair or a replacement. If you suspect the brand has generic problems, then ask for a refund.

Second, be firm. Once you decide on a fair and reasonable

course of action, stick to it. This decision will be a great help when you approach the seller; it will save you from stammering something out in a tentative tone of voice. Your indecision could encourage a cool refusal from the seller. Remember that the action you want taken is the basis for all further negotiations.

• Make a phone call or visit to the seller.

Ask to speak to the person who has the authority to help you. This probably means you'll bypass salespeople who don't have the power to make decisions on complaints. Ask for the store manager, the head of the department, or the consumer relations department, if there is one. If it's a small firm, ask for the president or owner. If you have established a friendly relationship with someone there, ask for him or her.

• Be confident.

Explain your problem firmly, clearly, politely, and without apology. Assume that a fair deal is possible; give the seller a chance to do the right thing.

• Make the seller reach an agreement.

Don't accept lines like "I'll look into it and get back to you." Ask him, "Whom do you have to talk to? Can you do it now? Can you do it by this afternoon?" Being firm at this point saves everybody time later on.

When you reach an agreement, restate it: "I can pick up the toaster on Wednesday?" "I'll expect the repairman on Friday at noon," or "So I can bring in my sweater and get another one exactly like it?"

Make a note of your conversation for the record. You'll need it if the seller fails to keep his end of the agreement or if further negotiations are needed.

• Set time limits.

Save time and effort by setting deadlines for a satisfactory agreement. Be polite but definite about this; after all, you purchased the product because you needed it. Don't let the seller think he can drag his feet. Even if your need isn't pressing, don't say so. Don't say, "Well, I guess I could wait until next month to have the bed fixed; I won't be having company until then." You have a right to have the issue settled promptly.

If you don't get help within a reasonable or fair period, then it's time to write a letter.

Do's and Don'ts of Consumer Responsibility

The Better Business Bureau of Metropolitan New York points out that consumers, like sellers, have responsibilities in the marketplace. Here are some of the Bureau's tips to help consumers play fair.

Don't:

- Complain to the whole world before you complain to the merchant.
- Crowd your letter with excessive detail.
- Be offensive or libelous in your letter.

Do:

- Know the terms of purchase when you buy something.
- Know the store policy on refunds, returns, exchanges.
- Be a responsible shopper: Keep records, comparison shop, be skeptical about exaggerated advertising claims.
- Keep a record of the name and address of companies you deal with (especially important in the case of mail-order firms or firms which advertise solely on television).
- Use gift certificates within a reasonable length of time.
- Think twice before making major purchases when you're away from home.
- Send a letter which can be easily read.
- Stick to the issues in your letter.
- Try to type your letter.
- Be honest in your reporting of the problem.
- Persist in a legitimate complaint.

Ten Consumer Commandments*

1. Know your budget. Evaluate "wants" versus needs.

2. Comparison shop for goods, services, and for the cost of credit.

3. Beware of impulse buying, in the food market and everywhere else.

4. Do not be lured by promises of easy credit. Payments are always hard to make.

5. Never sign a contract in a hurry. Read carefully every clause, including the fine print. Do not sign a contract you do not understand or one that has empty spaces to be filled in later. And remember: A consumer agreement should be written clearly. Always get a copy of the contract and keep it in a safe place.

6. Do not allow yourself to be rushed into immediate decisions for cash or on credit. The bargain that won't be there tomorrow may not be such a good deal today.

7. Read advertisements carefully. See if strings are attached to the promise.

8. Know the manufacturer's warranty and the seller's refund or exchange policy before you part with your hard-earned cash or sign anything.

9. If a business category is licensed in your city or state, be sure you deal with a licensee. Ask to see a license if it isn't on display.

10. If not satisfied with goods or services, don't despair. Complain!

* Source: New York City Department of Consumer Affairs.

The Effective Letter

• Be brief and to the point.

This isn't the time to write a short story; save the narrative for the kitchen table. Boil down events, remove excessive detail, and present the problem as economically as possible. Try to keep your letter to one page.

• Explain the problem clearly.

Make your explanations brief but full. Make clear what your grievances are and what has failed to be done. For example, the bricks are sitting in your driveway but the patio isn't built. Your car's been in the repair shop five times and still isn't fixed. The store manager refuses to exchange your sweater.

• Make a specific demand.

Clearly spell out what action you want taken. Don't bury your demand in the body of the letter or leave it up to your reader to guess. Put the demand at the very beginning or end of the letter; capitalize it; italicize it—just make it clear.

If there are a series of things yet to be done (steps in a construction process, parts of a car to be fixed), list them clearly.

• Include copies of all documents.

Include all relevant paperwork—receipts, bills, charge card bills. It is especially important to include a proof-of-purchase—the cancelled check, for example (*not* the check stub). Absence of this proof could give a company the chance to stall on action.

Never send originals of paperwork; send photocopies. You may have more than one document per photocopied page, but send photocopies in their regular 8 × 11-inch size. Don't send inconvenient and easily lost, smaller scraps of paper.

• Include basic information.

Make sure your letter includes all of the following pieces of information:

Your name (in the form used on the bill or as you use it regularly)

Your address and zip code
Your home and work telephone number (with area code)
The name and correct title of the person you're writing to *or*
    the correct department
The title of the company, properly spelled
The address of the company, with zip code
Full description of the product to make it identifiable
The date and place of purchase
Method of payment

• Avoid emotionalism.

It may be necessary for you to catalog a list of personal woes that the defective product or service has caused you, but do so as coolly as possible. Be polite and businesslike in tone. Don't sneer; don't be sarcastic. Don't name-call; don't use words like crook, liar, or thief. Rudeness—especially at the beginning of your complaint process—will not increase sympathy for your case, only reduce your chances for a fair hearing.

Not This

I'm so angry I could scream.

But This

I have a week's worth of laundry piled up because of my defective washer. With three children under the age of 12, this is an unacceptable situation.

• Locate the appropriate person to write.

If there is a consumer relations department, start there. A telephone call will give you the name of the appropriate officer. If there's no department designed to handle complaints, then write the store or regional manager. If this action isn't practical or if you don't get a response from it, then go to the top—the president or vice-president of the company, or the chief executive officer in charge of public relations.

In order to locate the name of the executive you should write to, as well as the address of the company, go to the library and consult

Standard & Poor's Register of Corporations, Directors and Executives. There's a new edition published every year of this handy reference work, which has an alphabetical listing of 40,000 corporations with their addresses and telephone numbers, and the names, titles, and functions of chief officers and directors. If you can't find the business you're looking for in *Standard & Poor's,* ask the librarian to direct you to further sources.

• Start the complaint process with the seller or manufacturer.

Some consumers make the mistake of bypassing the seller completely when they have a complaint, assuming that they won't get a fair hearing. But you owe it to the merchant to allow him a chance to settle things first. He'll be much less sympathetic to your claim if you take the problem to an outsider first.

If you meet with stalls, evasions, partial satisfaction, or a simple "no," then you should turn to third-party agencies to voice complaints and get action.

Locating the right agency to hear your complaint is simplified if you remember two points:

• Start locally, if possible.

You have a much better chance to settle a hometown dispute with hometown resources. Contact your Better Business Bureau, check "Consumer" in the white pages of your phone book, or call the attorney general's office. If you have a complaint against a licensed firm, call the licensing agent.

If you make a telephone call before writing, be ready to provide a short description of your problem. For example: "I have a complaint against a home contractor. Can you help me?" Don't launch into a long recounting of your problems until you know you're talking to the right person, then take your cue from his or her questions. Do yourself—and the consultant—a favor and be brief.

Be prepared to make more than one phone call in order to locate the right agency. Ask, "Which do you think is the best agency to handle this kind of problem?" And be patient; not everyone you talk to will be cheerful, helpful, or informative.

- ## Use the resources of *one* agency.

Many people make the mistake of "papering" everybody—sending copies of their complaint letter to a half dozen agencies. When an agency receives a copy of a letter that seems to be "For Your Information," it merely files the letter, assuming that someone else is taking responsibility.

Complaining simultaneously to a lot of different places may make you feel like you've covered all your bases. But agencies don't like it. You've only increased their paperwork—and yours—for no practical reason.

- ## Make your letter readable.

Your letter may be one of thousands that a consumer or third-party agency receives. Don't prejudice your case by sending an illegibly scrawled note on torn-off paper. Neatly print your letter or, preferably, type it. Leave plenty of margin space and keep paragraphs to a digestible length.

Don't write on dark paper that can't be photocopied. Don't write with dark ink on dark paper that can't be read.

- ## Make copies of all correspondence for your files.

Sources of Third-Party Help

Better Business Bureau

Better Business Bureaus are a system of 157 bureaus and branches in the United States which promote fair business practices, provide consumer information, and help resolve consumer complaints. Founded 70 years ago, BBBs are self-regulatory, non-profit agencies supported by membership dues and corporate contributions.

Unlike other consumer organizations, BBBs provide prepurchase information. You can call your local BBB and get information about a company before you do business with it. Your BBB has files on many companies (not necessarily BBB members) based on past records. It will share this information on the telephone or by mail, depending on the amount of information available. There are files on a wide variety of businesses—banks, charitable institutions, department stores, small businesses, and mail-order concerns, to name just a few.

About 60 percent of all consumer contacts with BBBs are inquiries of this kind. But the Bureau will also act as a mediator between a consumer and a merchant if the consumer wants to complain. Most disputes are satisfactorily resolved through mediation, but when necessary, legally binding arbitration may be used.

Local BBBs will also mediate complaints about local advertising. The National Advertising Division of the Council of Better Business Bureaus receives and investigates complaints about national advertising. (See page 81.)

BBBs prefer to have complaints put in writing. Your letter will be forwarded to the company involved and be used as the central document in their mediation of the problem.

Contact the Better Business Bureau nearest you (look in the white pages) or write: Council of Better Business Bureaus, Inc., 1515 Wilson Boulevard, Arlington, VA 22209.

Consumer Agencies

Consumer agencies run by the city or state exist in many areas. Some of these, like New York City's Department of Consumer Affairs, have licensing, regulatory, and law-making powers; others have more limited powers. If your local consumer agency has the power to suspend or revoke licenses, it makes sense to deal with it—your complaint gains clout if it could result in the suspension of a firm's license.

If you suspect that your local agency is small and overworked, give them a call and ask what kind of complaint backlog they have. If you think your complaint won't be processed quickly, use the agency as a referral service to find another consumer organization or trade association.

For addresses and telephone numbers of consumer agencies, look in the white pages of your phone book under "Consumer" or call your attorney general's office.

Newspapers

Some local newspapers have "hot lines" or "action lines" designed to help readers get action on consumer or citizen affairs. However, many newspapers only get help for the letters they print; others merely forward complaints to local government agencies. Newspaper hot lines aren't the most effective source of help.

Federal Agencies

If you can't get help at the local level, or if your problem escalates, you may want to contact a federal regulatory agency. In doing so, you will contribute to the vast amount of paper flowing through official halls—a somewhat discouraging prospect. On the other hand, you will also contribute information enabling government to write laws and regulate businesses which touch all aspects of our lives.

One agency which is committed to consumer protection is the Federal Trade Commission. The FTC investigates deceptive advertising practices, particularly of food, drug, cosmetic, and therapeutic devices, and unfair or deceptive business practices in general. It enforces fair credit laws such as the Truth in Lending Act and encourages truthful labeling of textile and fur products.

Consumers with inquiries or complaints are advised to contact one of the FTC's regional offices. (For their addresses, and the names and addresses of other federal agencies, see the list later in this chapter.)

Trade Associations

Trade associations are set up to protect and encourage the marketplace activities of an industry. They monitor professional practices and ethical standards of their members and keep an eye on the activities of the industry as a whole. Some industry organizations, responsive to their customers' needs, have set up consumer action panels to deal with consumer inquiries and complaints, like Auto CAP and MACAP.

Genuine responsiveness, of course, will vary from association to association. And remember, trade associations are interest groups; they lobby in Washington and donate money to candidates to encourage laws and regulations advantageous to them—but not necessarily to the consumer.

Refer to the selective listing later in this chapter for names and addresses of trade associations.

Public Interest Groups

These organizations, formed to protect and encourage the civil, legal, and consumer rights of citizens vary in their functions from litigation to research and fact-finding.

The names and addresses of selected public interest groups are listed later in this chapter.

Sample Letters

Automobiles

New Cars

Americans have a love-hate relationship with their cars. Some days, stabling a horse looks appealing when you fork over another hundred bucks for tires or spend an entire workday waiting in the shop. Other days, as you glide down a desert highway or up a mountain road, the automobile feels like the superstar of the twentieth century.

Tips for buying a new car:

Give yourself plenty of time to shop without pressure. Do your homework before buying. Automotive magazines like *Car & Driver* regularly report on the test performance of cars. The April issue of *Consumer Reports* is devoted to a report on automobiles. Comparison shopping is important when selecting a new car because the sticker price is often negotiable and because prices can vary widely with dealers. Go to established dealers who have been doing business locally for some time. Check with the BBB for a history of fair deals and prompt repairs. Be wary of salespeople who pretend to be operating against company policy. ("Gosh, my boss would kill me if he knew the deal I'm offering you.") Beware of oral "agreements" on such things as the trade-in value of your old car, options, and cash discounts. Get it in writing. Buy after the fall rush for better deals.

Even if you're well prepared and go to an established dealer, you may get stuck with a lemon. If your car looks like a lemon, first give the dealer a reasonable opportunity to fix it. There's no precise definition of "reasonable," but you might decide you'll stick through four or five trips to the service center, especially if the dealer is showing good will and a solid readiness to help. A recent New York state "lemon law" defines a lemon as a new car which cannot be repaired in four attempts or which has been in the shop a total of 30 days during the first year.

Careful documentation is essential if you intend to present a winning case. As suggested earlier in this chapter, you should keep a history of the car from the time you drive it off the lot—oil and gas consumption, problems, service and repair, and any complaints. *Be specific* about the problems and carefully log times and dates. Automobile problems can get complicated when smaller problems get swallowed up in larger ones, so keep careful records.

A letter of record and demand to the dealer puts him on notice that you expect responsive action within a reasonable period of time. If you want a refund on your lemon, say so firmly. If the dealer fails to respond, you can contact the car manufacturer, the FTC, or one of the industry's mediation agencies like Auto CAP (Automobile Consumer Action Panel). You can write Auto CAP's national office (refer to the agency list on p. 105) or contact your local Automobile Dealers Association, listed in the phone book, for the address and phone number of a regional office.

LETTER TO A NEW CAR DEALER ASKING FOR ACTION ON A LEMON

                              100 Adams Street
                              Anytown, U.S.A.   12345
                              July 1, 19--

Acme Showroom
Tom Smith, General Manager
Anytown, U.S.A.   12345

          SUBJECT: Year and Model of Car
                    I.D. Number
                    Date of Purchase: May 23, 19--

Dear Tom Smith:

My car is acting like a lemon. Repeated trips to your
service department haven't taken care of the numerous problems.
I demand a full refund of the purchase price.

Here's a brief history of those problems:

1. Rattle in passenger door at speeds over 25 m.p.h.

2. Gas consumption is excessive. (The car gets only
    18 m.p.g. highway compared to the estimated 29 m.p.g.)

3. Air conditioning freezes up and drips when put at any
    setting above 6.

4. Defects in the fuel injection system cause constant
    hesitation and stalling.

5. The radiator overheats and overflows at speeds of around
    50-55 m.p.h. Both you and your repairman, Jock Green,
    have told me this overheating is the result of "hot
    weather," but since we live in south Texas where the
    average temperature is 80°, I don't think this is a
    responsible reply.

The car is not fit for ordinary use, as defined both by the written warranty and by the Implied Warrant of Merchantability as set forth by the Uniform Commercial Code. The car has been in the shop 30 percent of the time since I bought it; its problems appear to be chronic.

If I don't hear from you on this matter before the week is up, I will place the matter before the manufacturer's mediation board or one of the automobile industry's appeal boards. Be assured that I will fight to get the refund I deserve.

Sincerely,

Used Cars

Double-digit inflation, rising unemployment, and the high cost
of financing and buying a new car have made used cars an attrac-
tive alternative. But many consumers feel their money would be
safer in Las Vegas than on a used car lot. "Would you buy a used
car from this man?" is used as an ironic comment on trust. In fact,
trusting used car dealers is not such a good idea.

Investigations conducted in various states show that dealers
rarely tell the truth about the mechanical condition of a car, and
most used cars have some mechanical defects. But most used cars
are only guaranteed to be serviceable at the time of purchase. That
could mean that if you drive the car off the lot you have no protection if you turn the corner and the muffler falls off, the horn
begins tooting, and the radiator blows up.

In 1982, Congress vetoed a proposed FTC ruling requiring used
car dealers to give consumers more information on warranties and
major defects. Meanwhile, some states are trying to put more teeth
into used car legislation. For example, the New York City Department of Consumer Affairs urged the state assembly to adopt these
guidelines:

- A minimum warranty of 30 days; longer for newer cars
- Expansion of inspection requirements
- Inspection and certification by independent parties (not
  dealers themselves)
- Results of inspection listed on window sticker with ap-
  proximate repair costs
- Disclosure of warranties in plain language on window
  sticker

If you buy a car from a new car dealer, you'll find slightly higher
prices but you'll get the advantage of on-site repair facilities, mechanics with know-how in servicing special makes, and you may
get a better warranty. Furthermore, you've got more option for
complaint, if you run into trouble. If you buy from an individual
and get a raw deal, your only redress will be to sue.

Tips for buying a used car:

Check the car out at an independent diagnostic center before buying. Test-drive the car on varying road conditions. Remember that high-mileage cars may be a higher risk. Check the car for signs of a major accident: repainting in patches, front-end alignment, etc. Check spare tire and tools. Make sure the car meets state safety standards before you buy it. Try to get an *unconditional,* full warranty for 30 days. Get all promises in writing—either in a contract or a warranty. Understand clearly all terms of payment. If a deposit is required, find out if it's refundable (get this agreement in writing, too). Ask for the previous owner's name. Call him or her and find out what major problems the car has. Check out availability of parts and service (even without a warranty). Keep an owner's record of service and repairs. Find out if your state licenses dealers. If so, patronize a licensed dealer.

LETTER TO A USED CAR DEALER

```
TO:        The You-Asked-For-It-You-Got-It Used Car Lot
FROM:      Mr. A. Customer
SUBJECT:   Automobile Make and Year
           Date of Purchase
DATE:      October 11, 19--
```

Dear Sir:

Perhaps I relied too much on your reputation as the largest used car dealer in our area, because when you told me that the above car was "in great shape," I believed you. I also believed you when you told me that the car had been thoroughly serviced and that there were no major mechanical defects. As you put it, "You may need a little adjustment here or there, but nothing to worry about." Well, worry is all I've done since I bought the car. Here's why:

● On October 1, the first morning I had the car, I woke up to find the battery dead. I paid $25 to have the battery recharged and was two hours late to work.

● On October 4, four days after purchase, I discovered a major problem -- excessive oil consumption. I drove to my uncle's house, 120 miles from here, and had to put oil in the car two times! On the return trip, I needed another quart of oil.

● On October 6, I took the car to Ray's Service Center to have its problems diagnosed. Ray's list (see enclosed service bill) includes worn valves, worn piston rings, worn bearings, and a faulty water pump.

● Also on October 6, I looked through the car's glove compartment and discovered the name of the previous owner, Mrs. R.R. Greentree of Smithers Lane. I called Mrs. Greentree and found out she sold the car to you on

September 30, only a day before I purchased the car.
Obviously this did not give you enough time to diagnose
or service the car.

• Between October 6 and October 9, I called your office
at least twice a day but was always told you were "out of
the office," "out to lunch," or "not available." You did
not return my calls. When I visited your lot on October 10,
you told me, "Look, buddy, you pay your money and you take
your chances." When I charged that you had misrepresented
the car's driveability and lied about its servicing, you
shrugged.

Clearly the car is not fit for its intended use, as described
in the Implied Warranty of Merchantability of the Uniform
Commercial Code. I DEMAND A FULL REFUND OF THE PURCHASE
PRICE OF THE CAR.

I will give you one week to make good on this before I notify
the State Office of Consumer Affairs, which licenses you,
and the State Division of Motor Vehicles, which receives
complaints about used car dealers.

Sincerely,

Auto Repairs

A few years ago, a Department of Transportation investigation discovered that out of every dollar put into auto repair 53¢ was due to inflated prices or unnecessary work. This survey confirms what many of us feel in our guts—that car owners are easy prey for unscrupulous repairmen. To many of us, the wheels, pulleys, wires, and thingamabobs under the hood are mysteries of the highest order. We don't know the names of these things, much less understand the basic systems of the automobile. No wonder we don't communicate well with repairmen, don't ask the right questions, and then agree to unnecessary work.

One self-defense strategy is simply to learn more about the way a car works. Check out the books in your local library, but go to the children's room or young adult section where you'll find some basic "how it works" information. Or you might take a course on auto mechanics at your local community college, adult education offering, or YMCA. Even if you never fix your own automobile, hands-on experience is invaluable when dealing with service stations or repairmen. At the very least, you learn the language and can substitute "crankshaft" for "thingamabob."

But all the knowledge in the world won't prevent repairmen from inflating prices by billing for more hours, a common practice among dishonest firms. To safeguard yourself you must find a reliable mechanic, one who will value your continued business.

Tips on choosing an auto mechanic:

Comparison shop for the best fees, hours, and for services like towing. Choose a licensed firm. Find a reliable repairman and stick with him. Take your car in for regular check-ups and tune-ups. Ask your mechanic for ideas on preventing problems. Talk to him; get him on your side. Don't let minor adjustments escalate into major problems. Get a written estimate of work. Don't sign the estimate before you understand everything on it. Ask the mechanic to call you to authorize work not on the estimate. Check the estimate against the final bill (which should be clearly itemized). Ask that a list of the hours worked be written on the bill, as well as the method used to calculate labor charges. If the repairman cites a flat rate manual as a source, ask him if he actually worked the number of hours noted in the manual. Ask questions.

When you're away from home and have car problems, follow these tips:

Out-of-city or out-of-state license plates are an invitation to some mechanics to get out their dirty bag of tricks. Be aware of such rackets as shortsticking with the dip stick, spilling oil under your car to simulate an oil leak, or substituting a worn fan belt for your own. Get out of the car and observe the attendant. Check the actual amount of gas on the pump against the bill. Stay with your car while it's being fixed. Lock up your valuables or keep them with you. Be aware of fear tactics used to sell new brakes, adjust tires, and the like. If possible, call the local BBB or licensing agent and check on the firm's reliability. If they don't have a good record, it may be worth finding another place, even if you must have the car towed.

LETTER OF COMPLAINT ABOUT AUTO REPAIR SERVICE

```
TO:     Department of Motor Vehicles
FROM:   Your Name and Address
RE:     Joe Smith, Owner
        Joe's Fix-It Shop
        Repair of (Make and year of car)
        Date of repair(s)
DATE:   August 2, 19--
```

I recently took my Hudson down to Joe's Fix-It Shop for repairs. The tires were veering sharply to the left when I applied the brakes. Mr. Smith examined the car and told me the problem was probably in the brake linings. He put new linings in and charged me.

When I drove the car home, I discovered that the tires still veered when the brakes were applied. I went back to Mr. Smith who told me the problem might be "front-end alignment." He said the only way to find out was to have the work done. He adjusted the alignment and charged me.

Since the tires still veered, even after this second repair, I drove the car to River City where my sister runs a repair shop. She told me I had been overcharged for parts and labor for both jobs. Please compare her itemized estimate with the bills from Joe's Fix-It Shop (see enclosed).

I think I have been ripped off, but I don't know what to do. I certainly have been overcharged on what looks like unnecessary work. I'd like a partial refund from Mr. Smith to bring the costs into line with acceptable business practices.

Sincerely,

Advertising

For advertisers, advertising is a form of persuasion. For the consumer who wants to make intelligent choices in the marketplace, advertising can be a source of information. Through advertising we learn about sales, new styles, new products, the cost and availability of goods and services, even how a product can be used. When advertising fails to function as a source of information or when it is downright misleading, we have a right and responsibility to complain.

Remember that advertising takes many forms. In addition to ads on television and radio, in newspapers and magazines, advertising appears on display ads in store windows, on matchbook covers, folded into packages, on billboards, on handout flyers, in direct-mail pitches, and with bills. And don't forget institutional ads which sell a public image instead of a specific product.

If you buy a product which fails to live up to its nationally advertised claims, you can write the advertising agency that designed the offending ad and send a copy of your complaint to the president of the company that made the product. To locate the appropriate people to write to, there are two handy books in the reference section of your library: (1) *Standard Directory of Advertisers—Trade Name Index,* and (2) *Standard Directory of Advertising Agencies.*

The first book lists 30,000 names of trade-name products and the 17,000 companies which produce them. The trade-name list includes such categories as luggage, apparel, automobiles and trucks, soft drinks, fabrics, games, hotels, household appliances, insurance carriers, paints, restaurants, shoes, sporting goods, and travel. For each company listed you will find its address and telephone number, the name of the chairman of the board, president, top management and advertising personnel, as well as the name of its advertising agency. The second book lists 4,000 advertising agencies, their key personnel, and accounts.

The Federal Trade Commission will review complaints about ads on television. For other national advertising complaints, contact the National Advertising Division of the Council of Better Business Bureaus, 845 Third Avenue, New York, NY 10022. NAD regularly monitors advertising on television, on the radio, and in print, looking for ads which are untrue, misleading, deceptive, or fraudulent and which make misleading statements about competitors. If you register a complaint with NAD, your complaint and the ad in question will be evaluated and the advertiser will be asked to substantiate the advertising claims. If it can do so, the case is closed. But if the evidence provided isn't substantial enough, the advertiser may be asked to change or discontinue the ad.

If the advertiser doesn't cooperate with NAD's decision, then the case will be referred to the National Advertising Review Board, which will convene a panel made up of advertising professionals and one public member.

When you submit a complaint to NAD, be sure to include the following:

- The brand name of the product
- The name of the company that makes the product
- When the ad appeared (e.g., the date of the print ad or the date and time of the television or radio ad)
- Where the ad appeared (e.g., the name of the newspaper or the channel and city of the television station)
- A copy of a printed ad

LETTER TO AD AGENCY COMPLAINING ABOUT NATIONAL AD

TO: Smith, Jones & Wright Advertising, Inc.
            1 Allen Avenue
            Cincinnati, Ohio   45215

FROM: A. Rose
            100 Adams Street
            Cincinnati, Ohio   45215

SUBJECT: Woosh Hair-Off
            Television advertisement
            Time of airing: Weekdays during soap opera
              hours (e.g., 12:45 p.m.)
            Place: Channel 8, Cincinnati (and other channels)

DATE: November 1, 19--

Television advertising for Woosh claims that the depilatory reduces after-use stubble; the implied claim is that you don't have to use Woosh as often as a razor. In the the ad, the legs of Woosh users are compared to the legs of razor users five days after use. The razor legs are said to have a stubbly texture; the Woosh legs are said to be "smooth" (free from stubble). The ad seems to say that all women will enjoy the benefits of Woosh.

I bought Woosh because of the advertising and used it according to directions. In fact, I left it on my legs the maximum amount of time recommended (15-20 minutes) in case my hair growth was heavy. However, the very next day my leg hair was returning as stubble. Woosh legs were not noticeably smoother than razored legs.

Will you kindly provide me with proof that Woosh advertising claims are true and accurate? Please tell me on what basis you claim that Woosh gives women stubble-free legs five days after use.

Thank you.

If you think a local advertiser is using deceptive strategies to pump up business and you can't get any plain talk, then contact your local consumer affairs office or the attorney general's office. When evaluating local advertising, look for misleading language in claims such as the following:

- "Going out of business." You can check with neighboring merchants to see if this claim is true.
- "Factory sale" or "warehouse sale." Does the merchant actually own a factory or warehouse? If not, the claim may be illegal.
- "Sale" or "discount." Are the goods offered actually priced below prevailing manufacturer's list prices or prices offered elsewhere? You should comparison shop to check this one.
- "Up to 20%—or 40%—or whatever—off." Ask to see merchandise which is being offered at the top of the markdown scale.

Another unethical practice is the "bait and switch" tactic. In this, an appealing special is offered in an ad, but when the customer arrives at the store the special is mysteriously "sold out" and the salesperson suggests the same type of product at a much higher price.

LETTER COMPLAINING OF LOCAL ADVERTISING

100 Adams Street
Anytown, U.S.A.   12345
May 1, 19--

Consumer Affairs Department
Anytown, U.S.A.   12345

Subject: Advertising Claim
Fred's Discount Clothing Store
123 Main Street

To Whom It May Concern:

Enclosed you will find a copy of an ad for Fred's Discount Clothing Store which appeared in the Friday, April 13 edition of the Town Gazette. The ad makes two significant claims:

1.   Merchandise is up to 50% off.

2.   There is a sale on pure silk blouses for $12.98.

I arrived at Fred's at 10 o'clock in the morning of the sale, Saturday, April 14. When I asked to see the silk blouses on sale I was shown a table of assorted blouses. Many were damaged, some were seconds, and many were fabric blends and not 100% silk. When I expressed disappointment over the advertised specials, I was shown a rack of 100% silk blouses for $49.95. This appears to be an example of the unethical practice of "bait and switch," luring customers with appealingly low-priced goods and then trying to "satisfy" that claim with higher-priced merchandise.

As to the second claim, I asked to see the store manager, John Doe, and to be shown all merchandise marked off 50%. This merchandise consisted of one table of socks, a small percentage of the store's total inventory. It was hard to determine what percentages the rest of the prices were marked off since they weren't expressed that way. But

Mr. Doe, when pressed, said he thought most merchandise was marked off 10% to 25% -- a far cry from 50%.

I'd like to lodge a complaint about what I consider to be dubious advertising practices on the part of Fred's Discount Clothing Store.

Yours,

Enclosure: Town Gazette advertisement

Door-to-Door Sales

The boy at the door is selling magazines. He doesn't bother to give you hard information about the diversity of his offerings or their low cost. He grins boyishly and asks you to buy three magazine subscriptions to help put him through college.

The man selling fire alarm systems sits in your living room showing you pictures of various models. Suddenly, he switches to full-color photos of third-degree burn victims. Without his alarm system, he tells you gloomily, this could happen to you.

Door-to-door salespeople are trained in the art of manipulation. They get into your house by pretending to know a neighbor or be taking a survey. They offer free gifts, praise your decorating, and get on a first name basis with your dog.

Of course, there are some nationally known and reputable companies that sell their products door-to-door. But many more salespeople represent shady or fly-by-night enterprises. Very often, those who buy from these people become hit-and-run victims, stuck with things they really don't want or things that don't work.

The best protection against being victimized is not to let these men and women in the door in the first place. If you do find yourself in the midst of a pitch you don't want to hear, be firm and hustle these hustlers out again. If you are interested in buying something, don't do so until you take time to read the material and the fine print. Ask the salesperson to come back later that day or the next morning. And ask yourself: Can I get these goods or services just as easily from a local merchant or by making a phone call? Chances are your answer will be yes.

If the salesperson agrees to come back, call your BBB and check out the company's reliability before he or she returns. If you do sign a contract with a door-to-door salesperson and wish you hadn't, you have protection under legislation introduced by the Federal Trade Commission. You have the right to cancel a door-to-door sales contract if you meet the following conditions:

- You must cancel *within three days* of signing the contract.
- You must send a letter to the seller informing him of your decision to cancel. You don't need to give a reason for your decision; the written notice is enough.

- You should, if possible, send the letter by registered or certified mail to prove you took the action.

The seller must:

- refund any money you paid in full or partial payment
- collect the goods within 20 days of notification

LETTER TO DOOR-TO-DOOR SELLER
CANCELING SALES CONTRACT

100 Adams Street
Anytown, U.S.A.   12345
November 1, 19--

The Fly-by-Night Writers School
Anytown, U.S.A.   12345

To Whom It May Concern:

I wish to cancel the contract I signed yesterday for a
52-week course entitled "Writing Humorous Fillers for
Fun and Profit." By law, I am entitled to a full refund
of the down payment of $19.95 (Trustworthy Bank #1123345),
which I expect will be promptly made.

The salesperson left a copy of the first workbook in the
course ("Grandmothers Say the Darndest Things"). You may
collect this merchandise any time in the next 20 days at
my address between the hours of 1 and 5 p.m.

Yours,

Food

Abundance, diversity, and competitive pricing are the great advantages of a free market economy. In supermarkets and grocery stores we usually have a wide range of products to choose from, from house brands to expensive gourmet food items. And the supermarkets have kept up with our increasingly adventurous palates. Meat and potatoes are still on the American dinner table, but so are fresh mangoes, tacos, *spaghetti alla carbonara,* artichokes, and stir-fried vegetables. Convenience foods are available in almost every category, while other Americans shun shortcuts and stick to healthy foods like whole grains, brown rice, and fresh fish.

Whatever your tastes in food, here are some tips for food shopping:

Be a prepared shopper.   Arrange your shopping list according to the layout of the store. Resist impulse buying. Don't go shopping when you're hungry or thirsty: you may end up satisfying your appetite in expensive ways. Try to leave the kids at home where they won't harass you into buying unnutritious or unnecessary treats. Try house and generic brands. Try new products if they fit in with your budget and life-style.

Resist sneaky appeals.   Recognize that no product by itself can make you prettier, younger, or smarter. Be aware of all-out campaigns by supermarkets and advertisers at holiday times. Remember that items marked "new," "improved," or "special" may not be any of these things.

Check the expiration date on foods.   Read the open labeling on packages. Often, this appears as the phrase "Use before (followed by a date)."

Read labels carefully.   Labels are a wonderful fund of information; don't be too lazy to use them. Labels list ingredients in descending order of amount. They will tell you if the ingredients in "health" or "convenience" foods really are healthy or convenient.

Labels also provide basic nutrient information and, on many foods, calorie content.

If you discover that the food you've bought is spoiled, crushed, short-weighted, overcooked or undercooked, or mispackaged (for example, all the strawberries at the bottom of the box were green and unripe), then return the merchandise to the store as soon as possible. If you can't bring the merchandise back (you threw out the chicken, for example), bring in the receipt and ask to speak to the store manager. Most managers will promptly refund your purchase price, in cash, to keep you a satisfied customer.

If you meet with resistance, or if you think the merchandise is just not a good product and you wasted your money, write to the manufacturer. If you'd like to complain about what you perceive to be unfair business practices (pricing, weighing, etc.) you can write to the BBB, your department of consumer affairs, or the licensing agent for the store.

LETTER TO A FOOD MANUFACTURER

```
                                     100 Adams Street
                                     Anytown, U.S.A.  12345
                                     November 1, 19--

The Delish Foods Corporation
Anytown, U.S.A.  12345

Dear Sirs:

Last week I purchased a 7 oz. package of tortellini,

filled with cheese, made by the Basta Pasta Company of

Milan, Italy.  The pasta is packaged and distributed by

your company.


I prepared the tortellini according to the cooking

instructions.  When I served it, the pasta was gummy and

the filling was gluey and grey.  It didn't look or taste

like cheese.  The tortellini was inedible.


Please refund my purchase price of $2.05 as soon as possible.

I enclose proof-of-purchase.


Thank you.
```

Furniture

Furniture varies from the inexpensive and utilitarian to custom-made pieces costing thousands of dollars, so it's the price that most consumers look at first when they're buying furniture. Next in importance is style, because furniture has to fit into your color scheme, current decor, and your taste—even if your rooms are decorated, like mine, in Early Eclectic. Cost and style are important but there are other important factors furniture buyers should consider.

Tips for buying furniture:

Look for durability. Is the frame constructed of long-lasting hardwoods? Or is it so flimsily made that it's stapled? (Cheap woods splinter when nailed.) Ask to see the underside of the construction. Is it well finished-off? Nothing dangling, unfinished, unraveling? Is the wood joined securely, with joints dovetailed rather than screwed? Check the padding on arms and backs of upholstered furniture—is it so skimpy you can feel the frame? Is the covering fabric dirt-, crease-, and water-resistant? Is it appropriate for the kind of wear it will get?

Read the label. The label will tell you if synthetics have been used to give the appearance of wood or leather and if the wood used is "solid" or "veneer" (thin sheets of wood pounded to ply construction).

Check out credit terms and delivery service. How can payments be spaced to your budget? What will it cost you to buy on credit? (Ask what the annual interest rate is.) What, if any, are fees charged for layaway? Are there charges for delivery or installation?

Get it in writing. Don't leave the store without getting the following in writing: (1) estimated delivery date, (2) full description of merchandise, including color, style, and fabric, (3) total cost including tax and delivery charge, and (4) complete credit terms.

When the merchandise arrives, check it thoroughly to see if it's what you ordered in every particular and if there are any defects or flaws in it.

The two most common complaints consumers have about furniture are late delivery and delivery of the wrong merchandise. After those, most complaints concern defective merchandise. Your recourse with late delivery may be limited to canceling the contract or negotiating a new delivery date (which still may not be kept). Retailers who must order from the manufacturer depend on the manufacturer's delivery date. Check when you buy to see if your merchandise is in stock or will be ordered from the manufacturer.

LETTER TO A FURNITURE RETAILER
CANCELING CONTRACT

100 Adams Street
Anytown, U.S.A. 12345
December 1, 19--

President
Homemart Stores, Inc.
Anytown, U.S.A. 12345

Subject: Rollaway Bed
Model #1234
My account number: 09 08442

Dear Sir:

This is to notify you of the cancellation of my
sales contract with you to purchase the above merchandise.
(See enclosed photocopy of contract.)

I ordered the Rollaway Bed on September 1 and was
promised a delivery date of no later than October 15. The
promised delivery date was written on the sales contract
at my request.

I bought the bed in order to accommodate the visit
of my late husband's favorite aunt. The bed didn't arrive
as expected, but Aunt Maude did, on November 1. I put Aunt
Maude in my bed and I slept on the couch for two weeks.

For the inconvenience caused by the non-delivery of
the bed, I have no real means of redress. But I would
appreciate your prompt attention to this matter.

- Please cancel the contract.
- Please remove the charge of $49.95 from my account.

As a formerly satisfied customer of Homemart for
nearly ten years, I'm disappointed by this failure of service.

Thank you for your attention to this matter.

LETTER TO FURNITURE RETAILER REFUSING TO PAY FOR DEFECTIVE MERCHANDISE

100 Adams Street
Anytown, U.S.A. 12345
September 10, 19--

The President
Homemart Stores, Inc.
Anytown, U.S.A. 12345

Re: Rockababy Lounder
     Model #1111
     Charge account number: 060841
     Date of purchase: July 1, 19--

Dear Mrs. _____ _____:

On September 3, my husband put our new Rockababy Lounger in the full recline position. As he did so, we heard a very loud spring noise, like a coil coming loose, and the lounger reared into its full upright position. As it did so, it catapulted our cat, Pickles, who was sleeping on it at the time, into the dining room.

Pickles was surprised but fortunately not hurt. However, the lounger is broken. It will not adjust to any of its reclining positions. Mr. Allen Winsome, your store manager, tells me that my two-month warranty expired on September 1, and that Homemart will accept no responsibility for the defective merchandise. While the warranty may have expired, this merchandise is covered by the Implied Warrant of Merchantability, which states that a product has to be fit for its intended use.

I feel sure that as a matter of good will you will PROMPTLY REPLACE MY ROCKABABY LOUNGER WITH A WORKING MODEL OR REFUND MY MONEY IN FULL. If you fail to act in this matter, I will contact a third party for mediation.

Of course, I will refuse payment of the lounger on my charge account until this matter is satisfactorily settled.

Thank you for your prompt attention to this matter.

Home Improvement

When it comes to home improvement contracts, a consumer's best defense is to be well-equipped with information before paying any money or signing anything. It is an area where mistakes are costly and the redress process can be long and difficult. So don't rush into a contract, and certainly don't make any spur-of-the-moment decisions about improvements. When you've decided what work you want done, it's a good idea to bone up on the subject— roofing, cabinetmaking, whatever—before you start. Then you'll gain a working vocabulary with which to talk to the contractors.

Tips for dealing with home contractors:

Comparison shop for a good contractor. Ask friends and neighbors for referrals. Work with a licensed contractor, if your state licenses this profession. Ask to see completed work (and if you visit the site in person, talk to the client). Pay as small a down payment as possible. Have the contractor provide you with manufacturer's warranty cards on brand-name products used in the work. Get proof that the contractor has all legal permits and necessary insurance. Get proof that all subcontractors have been paid before you make final payment. Beware of door-to-door contractors who want to do work with "leftover" material at suspiciously low prices. These workers may be legitimate, but if their office is a truck and their contracts are written on air, it's safer to steer clear of them.

Finally, make sure your contract includes all significant information:

- Complete name, address, telephone number, and license number (if applicable) of the contractor.
- Total cost of project. If this amount changes, so should the contract.
- A clear statement of beginning and completion dates.
- A guarantee against defects of workmanship in both labor and material.
- A complete listing of all items to be repaired or renovated (quantity, quality, brand name, model number).
- An agreement to clean up after the work.
- An agreement to dispose of unused material.

- If changes are made in the original contract while work is in progress, everything should be put in writing.

If you have troubles with the satisfactory completion of the work, speak to the contractor. Unless you suspect fraud or crookery, give the man or woman the benefit of the doubt to begin with. Contractors are often delayed by weather and by delays in the subcontractor's work. Be prepared to see a completed project which may not jibe exactly with your dream conception. Open up lines of communication between you and the contractor; listen well. But if carelessness, chicanery, or second-rate work are evident, then be firm about your rights. If you don't get a response from the contractor, contact your local consumer affairs office or the attorney general's office.

If your contractor is one of the 3,300 member firms of the National Home Improvement Council, you may turn to one of the Council's 54 chapters for mediation and arbitration. Different chapters have different procedures; some run their own independent arbitration panels, others work with the Better Business Bureau. Write the NHI Council, 11 East 44th Street, New York, NY 10017 for information, or check your Yellow Pages.

LETTER CANCELING CONTRACT WITH HOME CONTRACTOR

```
TO:      Better Builders Co.
         Anytown, U.S.A.  12345
FROM:    A. Rose
         100 Adams Street
         Anytown, U.S.A.  12345
DATE:    August 28, 19--
RE:      Work contract dated June 5, 19--
         Brick terrace and wall
```

Dear _____ _____:

This letter is notification of my cancellation of contract, effective today. Despite my repeated requests, you have failed to comply with the conditions set forth in the contract and with minimal standards of fairness and honesty. My specific charges are as follows:

- You have consistently underestimated the cost of the project, raising the price on two occasions. I signed a new contract on July 12 for $2,000 ($500 above the original cost) and on August 9 for $2,350. Now you inform me that an additional $250 will be necessary for the completion of the work.

- You have failed to correct the defective terrace steps, despite the contract guarantee which provides that defects in labor will be corrected without charge.

- You are running two months behind the estimated completion date.

Clearly, you have carelessly underestimated both the extent of the job and the seriousness of a contract which is legally binding. I expect you to stop work immediately, to clean up the terrace, and to pick up unused material according to the conditions stated in our contract.

Sincerely,

Mail Order

Mail-order catalogs were a boon to rural Americans at a time when trips to town were a rare occurrence and small-town stores offered limited merchandise. Mail-order advertisements appearing in magazines, on television, or in your mailbox are still a popular and established source of shopping for millions of busy consumers. Mail-order firms offer convenience, special merchandise not usually available elsewhere, and, sometimes, lower prices.

Tips on buying from mail-order firms:

Beware of extravagant promises.   Be skeptical of firms offering large loans, easy cash, overnight riches, "secrets" to instant success, and business opportunities which require no capital, no inventory, and no experience. Think twice about goods which seem to promise hair growth on bald heads, enlarged busts, the disappearance of wrinkles, or other miraculous cures for our human condition.

Read the language of the ad carefully.   A blouse may be described as "silky," "soft as silk," or be called "The Silkallure"—but not actually be made of silk. Careless readers may fill in what's left out themselves.

Notice what's left out in the ad.   "Too-good-to-be-true" offers probably are just that. For example, some mail-order insurance firms offer insurance coverage with incredibly low premiums or policies not requiring a medical checkup. But you may discover plenty of loopholes when you receive the policy—for example, it may not cover existing medical conditions or the premiums may rise sharply after initial payments.

Do business with established firms.   You've seen their ads for years? You've done business with them before? Then you improve your chances of getting what you paid for. Call your local BBB for more information about a mail-order firm.

Check the company's name and address.   Make sure its name and address are listed in full.

Most complaints about mail-order firms concern late or no delivery and the delivery of wrong merchandise. You can help avoid these problems by: (1) filling out the order form clearly and correctly, (2) listing your name, address, and zip code clearly and correctly, and (3) noting the promised delivery date. By law, firms must deliver merchandise within a due date, or if a date isn't given, within 30 days of receipt of the order. If the merchandise can't be shipped according to promise, the firm must inform the consumer and offer a refund, substitute merchandise, or issue a new delivery date.

The United States Postal Service is authorized to investigate complaints about mail-order companies. You can also contact your local BBB or consumer affairs department.

LETTER COMPLAINING ABOUT MAIL-ORDER MERCHANDISE AND ASKING FOR A REFUND

```
TO:      Better Business Bureau
FROM:    Your Name and Address
DATE:    August 1, 19--
RE:      Fat-a-Way Tummy Trimmer
         Slimjim Products
         P.O. Box 1000
         Anytown, U.S.A.  12345
```

I ordered a Fat-a-Way Tummy Trimmer on January 25, 19--, paying for it by check (see enclosed photocopy). Its cost was $19.95.

The Fat-a-Way arrived six weeks later while I was out of town. I began using the Fat-a-Way on April 2. Both the advertisement and the flyer enclosed with the merchandise instruct the user to : "Use the Tummy Trimmer for only ten minutes for ten days to flatten your stomach and have a trimmer, better figure. Guaranteed or your money back."

I used the Tummy Trimmer as instructed, ten minutes a day for ten days, but it did nothing for the coutours of my stomach. As a result, I returned the merchandise through the mail and asked for a refund.

That was on April 15. When I received no correspondence from Slimjim Products, I wrote again on June 1. Now the company has written me (see enclosed photocopy) and said I was supposed to use the Tummy Trimmer within ten days of receipt.

Two points: First, the literature doesn't say this clearly; it says for ten days, not within ten days. Second, I was out of town when the merchandise arrived. Was I supposed to arrange my personal schedule to accommodate Slimjim's shipping schedule? I think not.

The company has their merchandise back and I want a full refund of my money: $19.95. Can you help?

Thank you.

Enclosures: Check #00000
             Slimjim correspondence (photocopy)
             Slimjim ad and flyer

Record Companies

Most established retail stores selling records will offer you a refund or an exchange for a defective record, often within an unlimited time period. But if the store won't listen to your complaint, or if the record was a gift and you don't know the retailer, you will have to contact the record manufacturer. The record must be returned so that it can be inspected and exchanged.

Mail the record in a padded mailing envelope and include a letter which specifically describes the flaw(s).

- Which side?
- Which band?
    or

- How many inches from the outer or inner edge?
- What exactly is heard? (For example: a scratch, warp, blurred sound, etc. Try to be objective.)

LETTER TO A RECORD MANUFACTURER ASKING FOR EXCHANGE

100 Adams Street
Anytown, U.S.A.   12345
November 1, 19--

The Bigsound Record Company
Consumer Affairs Department
Anytown, U.S.A.   12345

      Re: Bigsound Album #123456
          "Songs of the Eastern Shore Birds"

I just received this album for a birthday present, but
I am returning it for exchange because of the following
defects:

    o Side 1, bands 1 through 5: scratch

    o Side 2, band 3 and band 7: occasional
       blasts of static which completely obscure
       the bird songs.

Thank you for your attention in this matter.

Agencies and Associations: A Selective List

Federal Agencies

Civil Aeronautics Board (Air Travel)
Office of Congressional, Commercial, and Consumer Affairs
Washington, DC 20428
(202) 673-6047

Consumer Product Safety Commission
Office of Public Affairs
Washington, DC 20207
(202) 492-5713
• Toll-free Consumer Product Hot Line:
(800) 638-8326
(800) 492-8363 (Maryland)
(800) 638-8333 (Alaska, Hawaii, Puerto Rico, and the Virgin
  Islands)

Department of Agriculture (Food)
Office of Consumer Advisor
Washington, DC 20250
(202) 382-9681

Department of Health and Human Services
Office of Consumer Affairs
200 Independence Avenue, SW
Washington, DC 20201
(202) 245-6296

Department of Transportation
Director for Consumer Affairs
Office of Consumer Liaison
Washington, DC 20590
(202) 426-4518
• National Highway Traffic Safety Administration
24-Hour Auto Safety Hot Line:
(800) 424-9393 (Continental U.S.)
(202) 426-0123 (D.C. residents)

Federal Communications Commission
Consumer Assistance and Small Business Division
1919 M Street, NW
Washington, DC 20554
(202) 632-7000 or (202) 632-7260

Federal Trade Commission
Washington, DC 20580

Consumer inquiries and complaints should be directed to the
nearest Federal Trade Commission Regional Office.

• F.T.C. Regional Offices

Office	*Region*
ATLANTA	
1718 Peachtree Street, NW	Alabama, Florida, Georgia,
Atlanta, GA 30367	Mississippi, North Carolina,
(404) 881-4836	South Carolina, Tennessee,
	Virginia

CHICAGO
55 Monroe Street   Illinois, Indiana, Iowa,
Chicago, IL 60603   Kentucky, Minnesota,
(312) 353-4423   Missouri, Wisconsin

CLEVELAND
118 St. Clair Avenue   Michigan, Western New
Cleveland, OH 44144   York, Ohio, Pennsylvania,
(216) 522-4207   West Virginia, Delaware,
                                    Maryland

DALLAS
2001 Bryan Street   Arkansas, Louisiana, New
Dallas, TX 75201   Mexico, Oklahoma, Texas
(214) 767-7050

NEW YORK
26 Federal Plaza   New Jersey, Eastern New
New York, NY 10007   York
(212) 264-1949

SAN FRANCISCO
450 Golden Gate Avenue   Hawaii, Nevada,
San Francisco, CA 94102   Northern California

Food and Drug Administration
Consumer Inquiries
5600 Fishers Lane
Rockville, MD 20857

Internal Revenue Service
Taxpayer Service Division
Washington, DC 20224
• Toll-free Telephone System
(800) 424-1040

United States Postal Service
The Consumer Advocate
Washington, DC 20260

Trade Associations

American Dental Association
211 East Chicago Avenue
Chicago, IL 60611
(312) 440-2500

American Medical Association
535 North Dearborn Street
Chicago, IL 60610
(312) 751-6000

Automobile Consumer Action Panel (Auto CAP) and *National Automobile
Dealers Association*
8400 Westpark Drive
McLean, VA 22102
(731) 821-7000

National Home Improvement Council
11 East 44th Street
New York, NY 10017
(212) 867-0121

Furniture Industry Consumer Action Panel (FICAP)
P.O. Box 951
High Point, NC 27261
(919) 885-5065

Direct Mail/ Marketing Association, Inc.
Consumer Relations Department
6 East 43rd Street
New York, NY 10017
(212) 689-4977

Major Appliance Consumer Action Panel (MACAP)
20 North Wacker Drive
Chicago, IL 60606
(800) 621-0477

Public Interest Groups

Action for Children's Television
46 Austin Street
Newtonville, MA 02160
(617) 527-7870

Aviation Consumer Action Project (ACAP)
P.O. Box 19029
Washington, DC 20036
(202) 223-4498

Citizen/Labor Energy Coalition
600 West Fullerton Parkway
Chicago, IL 60614
(312) 975-3680

Consumer Credit Project (CCP)
261 Kimberly Street
Barrington, IL 60010
(312) 381-2113

Attempts to end discrimination against women in matters of credit.

Consumer Federation of America
1012 14th Street, NW
Suite 901
Washington, DC 20005
(202) 737-3732

Largest national consumer advocacy organization.

Public Citizen
P.O. Box 19404
Washington, DC 20036
(202) 293-9142

Founded in 1971 by Ralph Nader.

Public Citizen Litigation Group
2000 P Street, NW
Suite 700
Washington, DC 20036
(202) 785-3704

A Ralph Nader group.

Suggested Reading

Consumer Information Catalog. Lists more than 200 selected federal publications of interest to consumers. Topics include automobiles, health, food, nutrition, energy conservation, money management. For a free copy, write: Consumer Catalog, Pueblo, CO 81009.

George, Richard. *The New Consumer Survival Kit.* Little, Brown and Company, 1978.

Gilson, Christopher, Linda Cawley, and Rick Schmidt, *Consumer Revenge.* G. P. Putnam's Sons, 1981.

Newman, Stephen, and Nancy Kramer. *Getting What You Deserve: A Handbook for the Assertive Consumer.* Doubleday & Company, Inc., 1979.

Nader, Ralph. *Unsafe at Any Speed.* Bantam Books, Inc., 1973.

Striker, John M., and Andrew O. Shapiro. *Super Threats.* Rawson Associates, 1977.

Verrett, Jacqueline, and Jean Carper. *Eating May Be Hazardous to Your Health.* Anchor Press, 1975.

Wrighter, Carl. *I Can Sell You Anything.* Ballantine Books, Inc., 1972.

6.

CITIZEN ACTION

One Washington story has been making the rounds for years. Whenever a senior senator from a midwestern state got what he considered annoying or just plain dumb mail from his constituents, he would write back something like this:

> Dear Sir:
>
> I think you should know that some damn fool has been writing letters to me and signing your name.

It's a funny story, and it features two cliches from the popular imagination—the backwater hick representing the electorate and the blustery, overbearing politician. Putting our faith in the democratic system, we can hope that this politician, arrogantly deaf to his constituents' needs, is a thing of the past. And we can certainly do our part as citizens to make our opinions felt clearly and persuasively.

Where to Go for Help

All legislators have one or more persons assigned to dealing with the problems of constituents. These constituent services are the meat-and-potatoes of any legislator's office, especially those that are on a two-year election cycle. In fact, some legislators get reelected solely on the strength of their constituent services, especially when their votes on issues are at odds with the sentiments back home.

What this means to you and me is that most legislators are very responsive to our requests for help or information. And while every issue will fall under the specific jurisdiction of federal, state, or local government, the practical fact is that some legislators will try to help you regardless of jurisdiction. If your legislator has an office in your hometown, make a call and ask to speak to his or her director of constituent affairs. You may be able to find out quickly where best to look for action on your problem.

U.S. Representatives. Congress is responsible for such national issues as foreign policy, the armed services, the draft, taxes, and the budget. In addition, congressional representatives deal with areas which are largely or in part federally funded but administered by the state. These areas include Social Security, unemployment, housing programs, welfare programs, and Medicare. Medicaid is also a state-run program. The Veterans Administration is a federal program. Immigration and naturalization are federal responsibilities.

State Representatives or State Senators. State government is responsible for such areas as ports and harbors; highways; driving and licensing vehicles; age requirements for driving, drinking, marriage, and legal status; public education and the school system; environment and water use; and health requirements and licensing for public services such as restaurants and theaters.

U.S. Senators. Some senators may be less responsive than their colleagues in the House to small or nitty-gritty problems. But their larger staffs and better resources make them a good choice if your problem deals with national or state issues (emergency aid to your hometown or region, state use of local water, etc.) Of course, you can voice your opinion to your senators on any state or national question.

City Officials. For areas such as sanitation, utilities, fire and police protection, city streets, and local schools, check the telephone book under the name of your city. If you live in a fair-sized town, you'll probably find city departments listed with addresses and telephone numbers. Or call your city councilperson or mayor. You may find listed under the mayor's office such helpful departments as: Action Line, Special Events, Community Affairs, Office for the Handicapped, and so on.

Note: U.S. Representatives and state legislators will usually deal with the problems and issues of the city they're located in. So even if a corner pothole or local bus service is not their legitimate concern, they may handle the request for action anyway.

How Your Legislator Can Help You

The majority of letters and phone calls to a legislator fall into two subject categories. The first consists of opinions on pending legislation, current issues, and newsbreaking events; this category includes requests (or demands) for the legislator to vote a certain way on a bill. The second category is made up of requests for help in dealing with government agencies, dealing with local problems (a nonworking stop light, garbage pickup), or solving a difficult personal problem (threat of eviction, service for the elderly or handicapped). These letters, called case mail, are often concerned with benefits—through Social Security programs and the Veterans Administration, for example. A third, and smaller, category of mail consists of requests for information on issues and laws and the legislator's stand on them.

When you send a letter to a legislator, his or her office will probably try to attend to it quickly. Some offices will start working on the problem the same day the letter is received. This helps the constituent and keeps the paper flow moving. If you mark your letter "urgent" or if your problem is in the emergency phase, you'll get immediate attention.

Good constituent representatives have ample contacts with local and state agencies and with the local branches of federal agencies. In addition, federal agencies in Washington have special units to deal with congressional inquiries. If your letter is case mail—a problem to be solved—the director will get on the telephone to one of his or her contacts. This person will try to track down the source of the delay or the trouble. "We can't change agency decisions," notes Nancy Cahn, who's in charge of constituent services for Rep. Bill Green (R-NY). "But we can cut through the red tape."

If you write your legislator expressing an opinion on an issue, inquiring what the legislator's stand is, or asking that he or she vote in a certain way, you will certainly receive a response. The more detailed and personal your letter is, the more detailed the re-

sponse will be. Your letter will then be tallied along with other pro
and con letters on the same issue. But will your legislator really listen to you?

First of all, it helps to be part of a chorus. If you are the lone
voice crying out for the return of Prohibition or for parking meters
in your one-horse town, your letter may not carry much weight.
On the other hand, if you make a careful argument for parking
meters, you'll have done the legislator a service by calling his attention to a need.

If your opinion—and others like it—coincides with the legislator's, he will use it to reinforce his position. "The folks back home
want this bill passed," he may say at a press conference, perhaps
waving a sheaf of letters. Numbers help in this case. You may have
noticed that the White House sometimes releases tallies of mail on
politically sensitive issues, if the numbers are on the President's
side. So if you want to give your legislator moral and practical
support, especially on difficult issues, write him. He needs your
backing.

But what if you are in downright disagreement with him? Well,
a legislator needs to know the size and shape of his opposition. The
loyal opposition gives him a more balanced sense of the issues. And
while legislators may not change their fundamental values, they do
change their minds. Elections, social issues, wars, the erratic economy, unemployment, and shifts in the public taste produce
changes which legislators respond to. Your opposition letter, if
reasoned and calm, is information your legislator needs, perhaps to
file away for future use.

How to Use Your Legislator Effectively

• Don't use your legislator as a first resort.

Unless you've got a situation which merits emergency action—
an eviction crisis, for example, or a missing Treasury check—go
through normal channels before contacting your legislator. Make a
reasonable effort to solve the problem with the agency involved.

Clearly, you don't write your legislator about the need for parking meters unless you've argued your case before the mayor, the city council, and community groups in your hometown. Similarly, if your Social Security check is a few days late, you should check with the agency first. Here are two further examples:

The Wrong Way to Do It

Mr. Big owns an appliance store on Main Street. He has just planned a two-week vacation to London to celebrate selling 1,000 washing machines. He wants to go right away, and, furthermore, he doesn't want the hassle of standing in line at the passport office. He's just too busy. Can't the congressman get this done for him?

The Right Way to Do It

Miss Trust applied for her passport eight weeks before her departure to the Galapagos Islands where she's going to bird-watch for a week. But the passport hasn't come and the passport office just says, "It's in the mail." She's worried. Can the congressman trace the truant passport?

In the first case, the staffer will probably gently advise Mr. Big to rearrange his schedule to accommodate the passport procedure. If she's feeling good-humored, she may tell him the best times to show up for the line and remind him to bring a book to read. In the second case, the staffer will call her contact at the passport office; eight weeks *is* enough time. If necessary, she will give Miss Trust information on how to get a last-minute passport.

• *Do* use your legislator to get information on procedures and policies.

The responsiveness of the staff to your inquiries usually reflects the personality and responsiveness of the legislator. But, in general, the legislative office can be a good source of information on government regulations and procedures. If that's what you need, make a phone call or letter your first step to find out how to apply for a permit, get a license, fill out a form properly, locate an appropriate authority, or expedite a process.

Office staffers are often a mix of professionals—journalists, lawyers, social workers, teachers, housewives—who can help a constituent solve a problem. In some offices informal legal advice is given; in others, sources of legal aid are made available.

When you call or write for information, check out all sources. Is there a recent newspaper article or editorial on the subject? A government or local pamphlet? Is there a staffer with special knowledge of the subject with whom you could talk?

• Don't use your vote as a bribe.

It's inappropriate to threaten or cajole your legislator. It's nice that you voted for him or her in the last election, but it doesn't give you special privileges (and it's not a provable fact, anyway). Likewise, your threat to withhold your vote in the next election isn't provable, and it's tacky besides. Even if you think your congressman is a donkey, your vote is not a carrot on a stick.

In fact, all you need to get help is to be a resident of the district or area the legislator represents. That's it. You don't need to be a legal U.S. resident, a registered voter, or a member of the legislator's party. Therefore, if you call the office, all you have to say is: "I am a resident of the 17th district and I need help on the following matter." If you write, your address will probably declare the legitimacy of your inquiry. (If you're not a resident of the legislator's district, your letter will be forwarded, as a matter of courtesy, to the appropriate legislative office.)

Note: If you don't know who your local, state, or national representatives are, call the League of Women Voters in your city. Information on the League's activities and voter information services is provided later in this chapter.

How to Write an Effective Letter

Problems or Case Mail

- ### Discuss one problem per letter.

This makes counting, filing, and problem-solving procedures easier. Don't make your letter a laundry list of national problems or personal woes. Keeping to one subject also helps you to be brief and to the point, the characteristics of a good letter.

- ### Include documentation and pertinent personal information.

Be sure to include your claim number, ID number, or Social Security number—whatever is needed to contact the appropriate agency. If you neglect to send this vital information, the resolution of your problem will be considerably delayed. It may be a good idea to send a photocopy of, say, your Social Security card.

Include your full name and address, apartment number if you have one, and both home and office telephone numbers. Including your daytime telephone number is very important in case a staffer has to get more facts from you.

- ### Don't ask for the moon.

Make reasonable requests based on specific goals. Don't ask your legislator to do the impossible, to change or bend laws, to put pressure to bear on other officials, or to act against his or her own best interests.

Opinion Mail

- ### Identify the issue.

Give the number of the bill or the name of the legislation. Be specific about an issue. Legislators are involved in dozens of issues under the general topics of taxes, government spending, unemployment, and so on. The more specific you can be, the more specific the legislator's reply will be.

• Explain your position.

To be effective, an opinion should have the writer's *whys* behind it. What do you think are the negative effects of a government program? What are the arguments against a new piece of legislation? What is the case to be made for a change in policy?

Don't say merely that you are for or against something: say *why!*

• Write from personal experience.

This is one of the best ways to explain your position. Many issues have a direct bearing on your life, your work, your family, friends, and neighborhood. Discuss these issues in personal terms and you help your legislator understand the practical consequences of political actions.

• Make suggestions.

If you can see a solution to a public problem, offer it in practical terms. Former President Carter liked to tell about a suggestion a state worker made to him when he was still governor of Georgia. The man worked mowing the median strip on the interstate highways. He suggested that only a narrow edge of the grass be mowed; the rest was to flourish as weeds and wildflowers. The state adopted this commonsense policy at a considerable savings of time and money.)

• Explain your expertise.

If you have professional, expert, or specialized knowledge of a subject, by all means share it. Your information may help a legislator better understand a problem or draw his or her attention to previously unthought of solutions. By the way, this advice doesn't apply only to big shots or people with academic qualifications. Many of us belong to special interest groups or have an insider's view of a situation. A working mother has something special to say about state child care facilities. A divorced father may have become an "expert" on custody laws.

• Time your letter.

If possible, send your letter to coincide with the introduction of a bill into committee or on the floor of the legislative body.

• Give praise where it's due.

A legislator's favorite letter? One which offers a thank-you or a pat on the back. When politicians are running for office, they get plenty of balloons and applause along with the chicken dinners. But the real life of politics places them continually in uncomfortable crossfire; they can't make everybody happy all the time. So, like anybody else, they like to hear deserved praise. A vote of confidence also gives them valuable feedback, especially on touchy issues. (Remember that "con" forces tend to be more vocal than "pro" forces.)

Special Tips

These come from Lisa Linden, Director of Constituent Services for Senator Roy M. Goodman (R-NY).

- Write legibly and clearly. Type your letter if at all possible. Remember that your letter is your image of yourself.
- Personal letters get personal responses; form letters get form responses.
- If your problem is urgent, mark the envelope "urgent" or "emergency."
- For real emergencies, send a telegram or a Mailgram. You'll get quicker attention.
- If you send a personal opinion written on company stationery, be sure to write "personal and unofficial" somewhere on the letter. Otherwise, the legislator may wonder if you're presenting company policy.
- Be sure to include your daytime telephone number in your letter. A staff member may need to reach you to get additional information.

Forms of Address

President
The President
The White House
Washington, DC 20500

Dear Mr. President:

Vice-President
The Vice-President
2203 Dirksen Senate Office Building
Washington, DC 20510

Dear Mr. Vice-President:

U.S. Senator
Honorable Joe Doe
    or
The Honorable Joe Doe
United States Senate
Washington, DC 20510

Dear Senator Doe:

U.S. Representative
Honorable Jane Doe
United States House of Representatives
Washington, DC 20515

Dear Congressman or Congresswoman Doe:
    or
Dear Mr., Miss, Ms., or Mrs. Doe:

President (Former)
The Honorable _____ _____

Dear. Mr. _____ _____:

Chief Justice of the Supreme Court
The Chief Justice of the United States

Dear Mr. Chief Justice:

Commissioner (of a Department or Bureau)
The Honorable ____ ____

Dear Mr. ____ ____:

Cabinet Officer
The Honorable ____ ____
Secretary of (Commerce, State, etc.)

Dear Sir or Madam:

Judge (Federal)
The Honorable ____ ____
U.S. District Judge

Dear Judge ____ ____:

Judge (Local or State)
The Honorable ____ ____
Judge of the Appelate Court (or other court)

Dear Judge ____ ____:

Governor
The Honorable ____ ____
Governor of (name of state)

Dear Governor ____ ____:

State Representative
The Honorable ____ ____
House of Representatives

Dear Mr. ____ ____:

State Senator
The Honorable ____ ____
The State Senate

Dear Senator ____ ____:

Sample Letters to Legislators

100 Adams Street
Anytown, New York   12345
November 1, 19--

Honorable Walter Brown
New York State Assembly
Albany, New York   12247

Social Security #000-00-0000

Dear Assemblyman Brown:

I need your URGENT help.

I receive a monthly retirement check from Social Security
in the amount of $306.20. But for the past three months
the check has been in the amount of $206.20. This looks
to me like a clerical or mechanical error, but the Social
Security office hasn't been able to track down the source
of the error.

My rent is $135 a month and I count on the remaining $171
of my Social Security check to pay for food, utilities,
transportation, and medical bills. I've had to dip into my
small savings to meet these expenses, but now my savings
are gone.

Can you help me? I need an IMMEDIATE check for $300 -- the
missing amount for three months. I need an IMMEDIATE
correction of the check error.

Thank you.

```
                                    100 Adams Street
                                    Anytown, U.S.A.  12345
                                    June 20, 19--
```

Honorable Jane Doe
House of Representatives
State Capitol, U.S.A. 12345

Dear Mrs. Doe:

Fairland Woods is a development which has been offering
decent housing at moderate rates since the war. My wife
and I, both teachers in this school district, have lived
here for nearly twenty years. But last week Fairland was
purchased by the development firm International Bigshots,
Inc., who plan to turn it into a condominium. We
residents are left out in the cold. I am writing, as
president of the Fairland Tenants Association, to ask for
your help.

IBI is an Italian-based company with international financial
interests. It doesn't know anything about local problems,
and it doesn't have local interests at heart. Nevertheless,
it is vulnerable, we think, to local pressure. We are
ready to put up a fight.

The question is: What kind of a fight? This is the first
major conversion in our area and we don't have much
information. What are the state laws on condos and coops?
Do tenants have any rights? What can we ask for? What
have other communities done in similar circumstances?

That's where we'd like your help. Will you attend our
tenants' meeting on Saturday, July 16, listen to our
side of things, and share information with us? Your
strong stand on housing issues makes you the ideal
person to help us challenge this international developer.

We look forward to hearing from you.

Sincerely,

100 Adams Street
Anytown, U.S.A.   12345
November 1, 19--

Honorable Tom Smith
State Senate
State Capitol, U.S.A.   12345

        RE: Proposed cuts to local library budgets

Dear Senator Smith:

I see that the above is among the items in the state budget
to be discussed by the Senate next week. I am strongly
opposed to any action which would cut library services,
perhaps reducing staff or hours.

Let me speak for the real importance of a library in a
little town like ours. As you know, Westfall doesn't have
a symphony orchestra, a performing arts center, or an
art gallery. But we do have a kind of cultural center, and
it's the Westfall Town Library.

Records, from classical to rock, are available to take out.
So are framed reproductions of art works. (I have a
rotating art gallery in my recreation room!) Recent issues
of magazines are circulated. The foyer of the library is
often a showcase for local talent in arts and crafts. And
of course there is a collection of Westfall history -- books,
old photographs, memoribilia, and old postcards donated
by local residents.
What about the basic business of book lending? Well, my
ten-year-old daughter Lisa is an avid naturalist, and I
don't know how she would have learned about birds, butterflies,
and salamanders without the reference works and field
guides in the library. My husband, Sam, who works in the paper

mill here, is studying auto mechanics with library books. I depend on the library for current best-sellers, detective fiction, and how-to books.

Your colleague, Senator Hornbluster, says that many library services are unnecessary "frills and furbelows." Are books, paintings, music, access to knowledge, and increased citizenship frills and furbelows? I don't think so. I think they're essential to the spirit and life of our town.

PLEASE VOTE AGAINST CUTS TO LIBRARY FUNDING.

Yours sincerely,

100 Adams Street
Anytown, U.S.A.   12345
November 1, 19--

The Honorable Bob Thomas
Office of the Mayor
City Hall
Anytown, U.S.A.   12345

SUBJECT: Rush hour traffic

Dear Mayor Thomas:

I work in the city but live in the village of Happy Valley.
I've listened to you on television and radio asking
commuters to use car pools or public transportation.
Neither alternative is possible for me, but, like you, I'm
concerned about the clogged traffic during rush hours. I
live with the congestion five days a week and see how it's a
time and energy waster, as well as being a daily source of
accidents, fender-benders, and overheated engines.

I have two suggestions that might ease the problem:

1. All government agencies (city, state, and federal) should
    introduce staggered work hours whenever possible.
    Schedules might be from 8-4, from 9-5, and from 10-6.
    This would spread out commuting hours, at least for
    government workers.

2. City businesses should be encouraged to introduce "flex-
    time," which permits employers and employees to arrive
    at flexible work schedules. The regular number of hours
    are worked, but the worker can make those hours in
    a four-day week or come to work early or late.

I know these suggestions would require a lot of work to
put into action. But as I sat stalled in a snarl of traffic
yesterday, they seemed like pretty good ideas. What do
you think?

Sincerely yours,

Resources

The United States Government Manual

This is the official handbook of the federal government, an invaluable guide to the agencies of the legislative, judicial, and executive branches. It's a short course in the bureaucratic functions of American government. It describes itself as offering: "A list of principal officials, summary statement on the agency's purpose and role in the government, brief history of the agency, including its legislative and executive authority, description of its programs and activities, and a 'Source of Information' section—consumer activities, contracts and grants, employment, publications, and many other areas of citizen interest."

The manual is published annually by the Office of the Federal Register and is available through the Superintendent of Documents. For information, write: Government Printing Office, Washington, DC 20402.

Federal Information Centers

Centers are clearinghouses for information about the federal government. Anyone having a question about any federal agency, department, or office in the government can call, write, or visit a FIC. There are Centers in 41 major metropolitan areas; 43 other cities are connected to the nearest Center by a toll-free tie line. Check the white pages for the FIC in your area.

Visitors to a Center will find government publications available, including consumer information pamphlets.

League of Women Voters

The League of Women Voters is a nonpartisan organization whose purpose is to promote informed and active citizen participation in government. It neither supports nor opposes candidates or political parties. Membership is open to all men and women over 18.

There are over 1,000 local Leagues across the country which offer forums on public issues, provide voter information, and sponsor candidates' debates. The League has become well-known for its nationally televised debates between presidential candidates. Some local Leagues also offer telephone information services and workshops in such areas as public speaking, parliamentary procedure, and running for local election.

The League also produces a large number of publications on local, state, and national issues. The publications cover such diverse subjects as women's rights, an evaluation of the UN, the balanced budget, presidential accountability, urban issues, housing, and how to pick a candidate. For a free copy of the publications catalog, which also contains further information about the League's activities and services, please write: League of Women Voters of the United States, 1730 M Street, NW, Washington, DC 20036.

Suggested Reading

Almanac of American Politics. Gambit, Inc., Publishers, 1982. Published every two years.

Congressional Staff Directory and *Federal Staff Directory*. Write: Box 62, Mt. Vernon, VA 22121.

Udall, Morris. *Education of a Congressman*. Bobbs-Merrill Company, Inc., 1972.

Who's Who in American Politics. R. R. Bowker Company, 1982. Published every two years.

7.

ON THE JOB

How to Start

One of the hardest jobs on earth is getting one. It's a process which requires organization, purposefulness, self-knowledge, knowledge of other people, research, time, and money. A sense of humor and an ability to roll with the punches are helpful. Nothing else will so much affect where you live, how you spend your time, your sense of self-esteem, your creative potential, your ability to be of service to others, or the money you have to spend—in short, your entire relationship with the rest of the world. The stakes are high.

This chapter will show you how to produce all the documents you need in getting (and leaving) a job, as well as some practical strategies for job hunting. Let me begin by pointing out what successful job hunters have known for years:

- Accept that job hunting is a full-time task in itself. A commitment of time and energy is necessary.
- Avoid personnel departments. They are clearinghouses for clerical and lower-echelon jobs and dead-end streets for serious job hunters.
- Identify the person within the company who can hire you: division or department head, manager, chief executive.

You can see that the essential characteristic of these suggestions is to get active. Merely mailing out cover letters and resumes and hoping for lightning to strike is far too passive a strategy—especially when high unemployment makes job seeking so competitive. After you've tacked the words *Get Active* over your desk or on

126

your bedroom mirror, put under it this motto: *Know thyself*—professionally speaking. Understanding yourself is agreed to be a generally good thing, but in job hunting it's a practical necessity, crucial to your success.

A good way to know yourself is to prepare an employment autobiography—an honest and detailed account of your job history. This history is for your use only; its purpose is to give you a clear picture of your experience and skills. From it you will select what you need to present yourself to a prospective employer.

One of the best ways to make this history is to get together with a friend, someone you trust and with whom you can be honest. Maybe you have a friend who also needs to straighten out his or her work history, and this occasion can be a mutual brainstorming session. Talking to a friend makes the job more welcome for many people, and your friend can ask questions that prod you into remembering important, but half-forgotten, pieces of information.

Make a worksheet, beginning with your first full-time, permanent job, even if it's far from your present field. If you're a student, a recent graduate, or have been out of the work force for a while, include all work—summer jobs, part-time employment, volunteer work, etc.

List the job by your formal job title, company name, and the dates of your employment. Then put down all the tasks you performed while working for that company. Next to each task, list the skills you used. Some tasks, of course, *are* skills in themselves—typing, for example. Since most jobs have daily, weekly, and sometimes monthly functions, that's a good way to begin. Then put down all occasional or one-time tasks. Include extracurricular activities, union jobs, committee work, formal or informal liaison work with other departments, even activities like organizing the Christmas party. Did you do any work outside of your field—design a budget, make an inventory, prepare a report? What about noteworthy achievements: promotions, citations, training programs, special assignments? Put them down.

These worksheets will give you a permanent record of your employment—but more importantly, you'll get a picture of your strongest skills. From these worksheets you can select what you need to produce resumes and cover letters.

Producing the Resume

A resume is a selective inventory of your skills and experience, not a complete history of your employment. It can get you in the door of a prospective employer or reinforce the substance of the interview once you're there. It's a personal document which you provide as a reference work for others.

As a personal document, the resume should look like a do-it-yourself project. Having an expert prepare your resume may be tempting, but writing it yourself will increase your professional self-knowledge and your self-confidence. By all means, use standard guidelines (I give you some at the end of this section), but rely on your own common sense and personal experience.

Naturally, if you're applying for a job in a conservative firm, you don't want to send out a resume that looks too original or whimsical. On the other hand, if you're in a profession where creativity is valued—advertising, some sales jobs, graphics, printing, writing, entertainment, communications—then originality might be welcome. For example, a resume doesn't *have* to be on white or off-white paper. Copy centers have a full range of colors nowadays—how about brown, rust, blue?

As for format, why not use a letter or memo form with very short paragraphs? Why not a list of your most impressive accomplishments, followed by a brief work chronology? Why not insert a short paragraph of an autobiographical nature to give a sense of your personal qualities? There's no law which dictates the form of a resume. All you must do is stress achievements (problems you've solved, skills you have) and make the document easy to read.

Your successes may have been brilliant, but if your resume is crowded, smudged, or filled with typographical errors, it may not get read. Some resumes are so black with copy they look like something cut in a cave wall. Use decent margins (say, 1½ inches all around), lots of white space, and healthy indentations. When you have the resume copied, make sure the reproductions are clear and dark. (Have the copy center run off one sample to see if it meets your standards.)

Readability is improved if you get your information across as economically as possible. Be sparing. Cut unnecessary words.

Make sentences short and sweet. Eliminate long, run-on sentences. Separate long sentences joined by a semicolon. Cut personal pronouns. (For example: Not "I managed the accounting office," but "Managed the accounting office.")

How long should the resume be? You need to include enough facts about your professional life and your skills so that your employer can decide if he needs you. If your resume looks thin or abbreviated, he may feel he doesn't have enough facts to base a decision on.

A one-page resume is usually too short for anyone with several years' work experience; two pages may be needed. Your resume won't be in danger of being too long if it offers concise and substantive evidence of your skills and value.

Don't put anything in your resume which would cause it to be easily discarded; leave out what is obviously negative or detrimental. The time to discuss such things as gaps in your work history is at the interview (if you're asked). On the other hand, you mustn't put in anything which would direct the reader toward an untrue conclusion.

Unhappily, distortions in resumes have become widespread. Maybe it's because when politicians and company presidents deal in large corruptions which make headlines, small "shapings" of the truth seem minor. Or maybe some job applicants take a purely coldhearted view of things: the marketplace is a jungle and any tactic is fair.

The ethics of such behavior is beyond the scope of this book. But there's a very good reason for not falsifying your background: you may get caught. You may not make splashy headlines, but you certainly may lose a job opportunity or create ill will at the very least. Remember, these documents might as well be written in stone once you send them off—they'll be a permanent record, a self-portrait in words. Unless you pull off your own Watergate heist, that record will always be available to anyone who wants to dip into the files. Keep it honest—while saving "confessions" for the interview.

If you do a thorough job on your employment history and put forth your strengths confidently on your resume, you should be comfortable about sending it anywhere. You don't need to rewrite your resume for each new prospective job. There are exceptions to this rule, however. You will need more than one resume if you have had strong job histories in two separate fields—say you've been both a housepainter and a kindergarten teacher and you're looking for jobs in both fields.

Here, then, are the most common elements of a resume:

Name, address, and telephone number.   List your work phone, if possible, but if a prospective employer calls at work, tell him you'll call back later—on your own time.

Job objective.   This entry tells the reader at a glance who and what you are. But if you want your resume to serve for more than one kind of employment, then omit this information. Listing an objective serves no function unless it's specific; don't put down something general or puffed-up like "creative growth potential" or "personal challenge." The entry can look like this:

Job objective:
Accountant *or* cost accountant *or* tax accountant

Skills.   You may wish to list your specific skills apart from the chronology of your jobs. This is especially helpful if: (a) you are making a career change and want to transcend your job category (say, from secretary to manager, or from manager to entrepreneur); (b) you've held a lot of job titles and want to emphasize a continuity of skills. Whether you list your skills by themselves, or in conjunction with your job history, be aware that your job title is less important than how well you performed your job. *Emphasize what you did, not your title.*

Experience or *Job/Work/Employment History.*   List the jobs you've held in reverse chronological order, beginning with the present, or last, employment. Include: job title, name of organization, city and state, dates of employment. In dating jobs, eliminate months and days: 1976–1980; 1980–present. Do not include the name of your supervisor or your salary.

Define your job responsibilities in terms of results: productivity, specific achievements, actions taken. Be selective—emphasize tasks and skills which support your job objective.

Education.   If you haven't received a degree beyond high school, omit this category. If you've made substantial headway toward a degree, list the accumulated credits, area of study, and expected graduation date, if known. If you are a recent college graduate and/or have degrees from very impressive schools, place this information at the beginning of your resume. Otherwise, save it for the end. An education entry might look like this:

Education

The University of Florida, Gainesville, Florida. B.A. in Education, 19--.
The University of Florida. 44 graduate credits in Special Education.

Memberships. This doesn't mean membership in the National Audubon Society or the local country club. This entry is for membership in professional organizations, especially those that have selective requirements.

Honors or *Awards* or *Fellowships.* Outstanding awards from college or graduate school belong here, as well as awards that recognize professional excellence or any citations which show you to be a good guy, or a good citizen, or a well-rounded man or woman.

Publications or *Papers* or *Presentations* or *Talks.* Entries might look like this:

"Hope for the Inner City." Op-Ed article in *The Houghtonville Times,* March 16, 1976.
"The Banker's Dilemma." Talk given to the Houghtonville Chamber of Commerce, January 4, 1979.

Here are other resume entries which you may or may not want to include:

Activities. There is no reason to include this entry unless your interests are out-of-the-ordinary. It doesn't distinguish you to mention swimming, reading, theater, or cooking. But if you're an amateur expert on World War I or take an annual cross-country bicycle trip, then say so. A writer friend of mine collects butterflies and volunteers his time at a university's entomology department; that kind of commitment is worthy of note. By the way, don't call this entry "Hobbies." Children have hobbies; adults have avocations.

Marital status. Include this entry only if it benefits you. If being a family man or woman would appeal to an employer or explain why you've been out of the job market for a while, then it's a help to put down "Married, two grown children." On the other hand, while "divorced" may mean independence to you, it may represent something less positive to a boss (banks, for example, perceive divorced customers as less good risks for credit cards than married people.)

Age.   If you've listed the date you graduated from college, this entry isn't necessary. Otherwise, the date of your birth may be placed after your name and address. Like it or not, people are curious about your age, and a boss has a legitimate interest in you as a product of a particular generation.

Physical description.   Your height, weight, and state of health are only appropriate if you're a model or a wrestler. Usually, these facts are completely irrelevant to your ability to perform a job. In addition, the "best" resumes leave them out nowadays; your resume may look old-fashioned if you include them.

Finding the Jobs

When you have finished your resume, you are ready to contact prospective employers. In some cases, you will look for existing job openings and so your search may begin with newspaper ads, employment agencies, or finding out about vacancies. But in other cases, you will contact employers and institutions for whom you want to work—even if you don't know of an opening.

Paradoxically, this second strategy is the most efficient. It has two immediate advantages. First, it doesn't depend on accident— the perfect job being vacant at the perfect time. A second advantage is that you will be the sole applicant! In this way, you avoid competing with dozens, perhaps hundreds, of other job seekers.

If this is a new idea to you, I suggest you read Richard N. Bolles's wise and useful book, *What Color Is Your Parachute?* (Ten Speed Press, 1983). Bolles's guide for job-hunters and career-changers points out that an organization may have an as-yet-undiscovered job opening for the following reasons:

1. The organization is expanding and it is gong to need *more* of what it already has plus *new* skills.
2. The organization is reducing its staff, but still may need *one* generalist with many skills to replace *several* previous slots.
3. Even in organizations which are neither growing nor cutting back, there are always old, unsolved problems or new ones cropping up everyday.

Organizations are not monoliths; they are more like rivers. They have forward-going places, but they also have swirling eddies, rapids, standing swamps, and backwaters. The person who can identify the changing waters and/or help control the flow has a chance of getting a job.

In their book *Getting to Yes,* Roger Fisher and William Ury point out that when people try to negotiate something—a divorce contract, for example, or a labor dispute—they generally take one of two positions. One, they assume that the participants in the negotiation are friends and seek an agreement. Or, two, they assume that the participants are adversaries and seek a victory. Fisher and Ury suggest a better assumption: *Participants are problem-solvers. They seek a solution to a problem.*

It may be helpful to keep this thought in mind during your job hunt. Your prospective employer is neither a person to befriend nor an enemy to be feared. He or she is a person with a problem. The problem may be a specific job vacancy, or it may be a nagging cost overrun, low productivity, or bad public relations. In any case, if you can solve the problem, you may have a job.

Here are the essential steps in finding—and reaching—the institutions and organizations you want to work for.

• Do research.

The first stop is the reference section of the library where there are hundreds of sources giving information on American businesses, whether the business provides goods or services. These are some good ones (the librarian can suggest more):

Dun & Bradstreet's Million Dollar Directory
F & S Index of Corporations and Industries

The Foundation Directory
Standard & Poor's Register of Corporations, Directors, and Executives
Who's Who in Commerce and Industry

• Ask your librarian.

A growing number of libraries have job information centers, containing both circulating and reference books, vertical file materials, pamphlets, and bibliographies. In other libraries, you can find career information in the business section. Talk to the librarian; tell him what you're looking for. (And ask him to steer you to the books and authors with good reputations and credibility.)

• Create your own resource files.

As you research a company which interests you, begin to build a portfolio on it. Learn as much as you can about its history, procedures, products, services, public image, growth potential, and the people who run it. In addition to reference books, good sources for this information are the business pages of *The New York Times* and your local newspaper, magazines such as *Business Week, Forbes, Fortune,* and *The Wall Street Journal,* as well as trade publications and annual reports.

Don't forget to get help from people—talk to friends, relatives, co-workers, former colleagues, your dentist, and your tax accountant. You can sometimes get a fund of information—even contacts—from an unexpected source.

• Identify the person who can hire you.

While you're accumulating for yourself a set of facts about prospective workplaces, you will also be on the lookout for the names and titles of people who can hire you. When in doubt, aim high. If you're not sure which division or department to apply to, contact a vice-president. If the company is small, go to the president.

If that action seems presumptuous, think of this: Every new workday, the president is faced with a new crop of questions needing creative, practical and specific answers. He wants those answers. And since company presidents love to talk about their companies, you're an ideal listener—a stranger who's knowledge-able. (You've done your homework, haven't you?) He may be just as glad to talk to you as you are to him.

And remember, the president—unlike those under him—isn't likely to feel threatened by a job-seeker. You're not after *his* job, after all.

• Identify the movers and shakers.

This is another good way to find the person who can hire you. Regularly read the business news in newspapers, magazines, trade and professional journals, and watch out for success stories. Who's recently gotten a promotion, a new position, a new assignment? New jobs mean new responsibilities—and that may mean new staff appointments. What individuals—and divisions—are being cited for achievement, are being talked about in the industry? Successes often encourage money flow and increased staff.

• Go on information interviews.

You can continue your research right through the doors of the company you're interested in—by going on an information inter-view. The purpose of this interview is simply to get a closer look at the company and to find out if your skills and background match up with their needs. Could you contribute? Do you feel comfort-able? Are your styles in sympathy? If you're a button-down person, will you be at ease in a world of blue jeans? (On the other hand, there's no law against diversity.)

The information interview is not a job interview. It's a much more relaxed situation for both you and the employer. As Richard Bolles points out in *What Color is Your Parachute?*, it is a low-stress form of window-shopping. While you're getting important infor-mation about the company, the employer can informally check you out.

The best way to ask for an information interview is on the tele-phone, not with a letter. If you write a letter, you'll just have to follow it up with a phone call. So, take courage and call. You may get stopped with a secretary's queston: "Does he know what this is in reference to?" Don't say "no," just reply: "I'm calling to request information" or "I'm interested in learning more about American Widget."

If telephoning makes you nervous, or if you're requesting an interview in another town, then write a letter. Follow up the letter with a phone call within a week.

Whether you write or call, be brief and to the point. Suggest a possible time span for the interview (e.g., "the week of the 27th"). Be specific about the amount of time you'll need—don't let your contact be afraid he'll have to spend half a day with you. Twenty minutes is about right for a busy, successful person. (Once you're at the interview, end it on time even if it's going well. You'll get clear signals from your contact if he wants to continue talking.)

Here are the essentials of a letter requesting an information interview. (See the sample letters on pages 154–155.)

Note: Take along a resume with you when you go for the interview. Information interviews sometimes turn into job interviews.

```
        I am not looking for a job at present.  But
I am exploring work options (looking into career
possibilities) in my profession which is management
(or accounting or personnel).

        I've done some research on your organization
(I've been reading about your company) and I'm interested
in the kind of work it does.  May I make an appointment
to see you for about twenty minutes?

        I'll call you soon to set up a time convenient
to you.
```

• **Keep records.**

You should keep records of *all* transactions between yourself and an employer or organization. Don't count on your memory for this; you need an accurate facts-on-file for each organization you contact. (And be sure to get names of secretaries and list contacts with them. Secretaries are often as well-informed as their bosses, and they have the power to give—and withhold—access to the inner office. Remembering their names is more than a courtesy; it's good politics.)

Besides recording the dates, times, and subject matter of all contacts, the most important thing you can do is to record the feeling or tone of the meeting as well as stray bits of specific information. Was the meeting friendly, relaxed, informative, or strained? Will this person help you again or is he apt to give you the brushoff? Anything could be useful to you in future correspondence. (Haven't you sometimes wished you had recorded the names of the children of former colleagues, for example? Then you're not stuck with: "And how's your beautiful daughter, what's-her-name?")

While you should keep these kinds of records to ease your job search, you *must* keep them for tax purposes. The expenses of job hunting—transportation, for example—are deductible; see your tax accountant about this. But meanwhile: *Keep accurate records.*

Writing the Cover Letter

A cover letter, which accompanies a resume, has one objective: to get an interview. Its chief functions are to introduce you and name the position you want. It may also say why you are qualified for the position and refer to the resume for specific examples.

A cover letter allows you to speak directly to your prospective employer. It's a personal expression, however brief. While the resume represents a broad range of experience, the cover letter selects and presents specific facts advantageous to you.

The letter should create a climate of good will. Be confident but not arrogant, natural-sounding but not presumptuous or chatty. You are speaking on your own behalf with neither timidity nor grandiosity.

The cover letter and resume are sometimes referred to as a "sales brochure" or "selling tool." This language may be helpful in prodding the reluctant job-seeker into being more hard-hitting. But there are dangers in thinking of yourself as the object of a sales pitch.

First, you may get too concerned with the packaging and not the substance. Remember, your best selling tools are a knowledge of your skills and a knowledge of the company you want to work for. Second, you don't want to get attention by appearing too pre-packaged. Avoid being self-conscious; speak naturally and directly. Don't make yourself look like a glossy commodity; bosses may be suspicious that there's nothing underneath the gloss and glitter.

Let's begin looking at a typical cover letter:

```
Dear Ms. Green:

Enclosed please find my resume.  I'm certain that after
reading it you'll agree I'd be a valuable addition to
your staff.

I have not been challenged to my full capacities since
joining my present company.  As a result I am seeking
a change.

I look forward to hearing from you.  I can be reached
during the evenings and weekends at 555-8642.
```

Almost everything is wrong with this letter. It has a boring, pre-dictable opening. It presumptuously draws unwarranted conclu-sions: "I'm certain you'll agree" and "I'd be a valuable addition." The letter writer can't know what Ms. Green will conclude on reading his resume; he must give strong evidence that he can be of value to her organization. He can't do that because he fails (a) to address the concerns of the company and (b) to give specific in-stances of his own achievements.

He's not specific, either, about the kind of challenge he wants. Challenge is one of those wonderful words that has a stirring ring to it, but means little unless it's grounded in specifics. And why hasn't the letter writer created his own challenges—did he work for a company that had no problems that needed solving? "Seeking a change" sounds commendable—but doesn't he simply mean a new position? If so, he should say so—and name the position he wants.

Finally, he suggests that the employer do all the work—he'll just wait to be phoned. And what's more, he wants to be phoned on the employer's personal time.

The letter is passive, routine, and full of generalizations, qualities that are guaranteed to get it—and the resume—chucked out without a second glance. Here's how to write a cover letter which will get your resume read, and get you an interview.

• Emphasize what you can do for an organization.

In letters and in interviews, job-seekers often try to impress by stressing their eagerness and willingness to work. But that's a little like going into Tiffany's and hoping to get a bracelet because you're enthusiastic about emeralds.

These job-seekers misguidedly keep the focus on themselves and on what *they* want. They use "selfish" language as in the following examples.

Don't Do This

1. "I have just received six weeks of training on a Vydec word processor and am eager to begin working."

2. "I'd like to work for your company because the field of education has always interested me."

3. "I am interested in working for a company where I use my full capacities and gain hands-on experience."

4. "I am anxious to learn all phases of personnel work."

5. "I'm looking for an organization that can appreciate my skill as a problem-solver."

Instead of focusing on what you *want*, focus instead on what you've *done* and, therefore, what you can do for the company. Whenever possible, address its specific needs and concerns. *Show that you've done your homework,* that you understand the language and problems of the organization.

Do This

1. "I have been trained on a Vydec, have good typing ability, excellent organizational skills, and like to work with details. May I talk to you about the role word processing plays in the field of telecommunications?"

2. "I have a strong advertising background and I'd like to share with you some of my ideas for using advertising strategies for your student recruitment program."

3. "I want to work for a company like American Widget, with its reputation for growth, so that I can use my hands-on experience in designing successful marketing campaigns."

4. "I'm results-oriented, articulate, and highly motivated. And my three years in sales have taught me to be a quick learner."

5. "I like to solve problems. May I share with you some of my ideas for fund-raising in tight-money times?"

• Be specific about your achievements.

It's not enough to claim that you are "a self-starter," "an innovator," "a successful manager"; that you have "well-rounded experience," "a talent for organization," or "broad capabilities"; that you can "communicate effectively" or "increase revenues." You should back up general statements about your worth with specific instances of achievement.

If you say you're a self-starter, then give evidence of your independence and initiative. Perhaps, on your own, you solved a chronic paper-flow problem, started a staff newsletter, figured out a better way to reach clients, began your own local radio show, or initiated a speakers series for the PTA. If so, say so.

An excellent way to be specific is to describe *results*. If the action you took produced measurable or observable results, highlight them. As a book dealer, you created a videotape as part of your selling presentation. Result: 20 percent more orders. As the publicity coordinator for the Chamber of Commerce, you wrote an original slogan for the city and had it printed on stickers. Result: a plug for the city in every store window.

• Create strong openings.

Ruth Shapiro, president of a New York-based career development firm, suggests opening a cover letter with a strong accomplishment relevant to the job you're seeking. For example:

"As a direct result of procedures I have instituted here at Morgan Industries, absenteeism is down by 10% and productivity is up 20%."

"As a real estate agent who did half a million dollars worth of business last year, I have to have a clear understanding of the money market. I'd be an ideal candidate for the management trainee program in your investment house."

Dropping a name is another effective opening. Name-dropping won't get you a job, but the right name can be good public relations for you and ease your introduction to the reader.

"Bob Highland has told me about the work you're doing in communications. It's work I'm strongly interested in, since I redesigned my division's computer program, reducing paper duplication by 32%."

"Barbara Hall, Vice-President of Patmore Productions, worked with me last year on the Muscular Dystrophy Fund Drive. She suggested that you have openings in your department from time to time for a copywriter. I have five years' experience producing educational and promotional brochures in the field of medical advertising."

If your reference knows your worth well enough to recommend you, or pay you a compliment, say so.

"Bill Hanson tells me you may have an opening for a senior accountant on your staff, and thinks I might have just the collection of skills and experience you're looking for."

Another strategy is to open with an attention-getting or unusual one-liner. Use this strategy only if you're comfortable with your creative abilities. (There's nothing worse than cleverness that doesn't work.)

"What do trouble-shooting on the Alaska pipeline and investment banking have in common?"

"Bill Tice says I'm the best damn copywriter he's got and he'd hate to lose me."

"Mother always told me that nice girls finish last. But she didn't know I was going to grow up to be Fabbrico's Salesperson of the Year."

- ## Apply for only one position.

There are still some job-hunters who earnestly—and naively—write this kind of thing to a prospective employer:

> "I am willing to accept any position which will give me a chance to learn."

There are several good reasons why you shouldn't do this. First, it's a very passive technique; it asks someone else to figure out what's best for you. Second, it shows a lack of professional self-knowledge. Finally, it's insincere. Does the job-hunter really mean *any* job? Accountant? Janitor? If the job-hunter means he'll be glad to start at the bottom, he ought to be aware that one man's "bottom" is another man's job. For example, the custodian's job has very specific requirements and responsibilities; it may look like "anything" to someone else, but not to the person who has it.

You should have a clear-cut employment goal for each employer you write to. Of course, your job objective may change from employer to employer (e.g., from "writer" to "copywriter"). But never ask the employer to figure out what you can do best. It's not his responsibility and he won't do it to your advantage.

- ## Use language natural to you.

You don't have to use a special, "business" English for cover letters or exhibit a talent for stylish, creative writing (unless, of course, you're trying for a job using writing skills). Imagine that you are speaking directly to someone, not writing. Focus on what you're saying, not how you're saying it.

- ## Use words that convey action and skills.

Before you dip into this list, be certain that the words you choose actually match the activities you have performed. Don't be like the ad writer who described a plastic sugar bowl as "engineered for efficiency." (Bridges are engineered, not plastic sugar bowls.)

initiated	originated
created	conceived

established	managed
built	superintended
made	directed
assembled	headed
prepared	guided
produced	represented
designed	instructed
devised	taught
developed	informed
organized	explained
coordinated	persuaded
arranged	interpreted
supervised	wrote
conducted	edited

- ## Use the active, not the passive, voice.

  Passive: Was selected to represent . . .
  Active: Represented the company at the annual Chamber of Commerce Awards Luncheon.

  Passive: The report was prepared by myself and my staff.
  Active: I prepared the report with the help of my staff.

- ## Keep the action in your court.

  Don't expect your reader to do anything but read your documents—the letter and/or resume—with an open mind. That's action enough—in fact, it's plenty.

  You are the actor in these transactions: you take action, initiate proceedings, and you keep things going. You don't sit passively waiting for the phone to ring. If it does—and this sometimes happens, if a company has an opening and you're exactly right for it—that's great. But you're not a girl hoping for a date. You're a job-hunter with serious business at hand. You're an activist.

- ## Request an interview.

  Ask for an interview by saying *you* will telephone. Then do it.
  If it's long-distance, remember: it's worth the money to keep the action in your court.

- ## Revise for clarity.

Type the first draft of your cover letter so you can see how it looks "in print" and how it looks on the page. Then go over your rough draft and cut for the sake of clarity. Omit any words, phrases, or sentences that do not tend to support your objective of getting an interview. Hack away at wordiness or pretentious language. Refer to the section on wordiness on page 30. Cut out overused words, cliches, and jargon. It's almost always safer to be too short than too long.

- ## Make the letter easy to read.

Avoid long run-on sentences and big fat paragraphs. Short paragraphs, moderate sentence length, lots of white space, and big margins will encourage readability. When you've typed the letter, look at it with an editor's eye: Does it look like an invitation or a dissertation?

- ## Opt for brevity.

Remember, not every job is hard to get. If you're a first-rate word processor, nurse, secretary (or any of the other job categories which are underemployed at this writing), you don't need a hard sell. Your resume is your most persuasive document.

It's acceptable, in those circumstances, to send a letter like the following:

```
Dear Mr. Smith:

I'd like to be considered for the position of cost
accountant with Rayco Industries.  In the enclosed resume
you'll find a full history of my experience.

I'll call you next week for an appointment.

Thank you.
```

Couldn't be done, you say? It looks somehow forlorn, like a newly shorn sheep on a windy hill? It's just too short! It *is* short, but it mentions a specific job title and requests an interview. Also, it mentions the company's name and makes reference to a job history documented in the resume. What would an employer think? Well, he reads fat, long-winded memos and letters all week; he might be grateful for some leanness in presentation.

What *Not* to Do in a Cover Letter

- ### Don't be negative.

Stress positive achievement and emphasize strengths. As with the resume, the cover letter is not the place to explain, apologize, or rationalize. Leave explanations for the interview.

- ### Don't mention salary.

If you're too specific about salary on paper, you may box yourself into a lower scale. If you're too broad (e.g., "in the $20,000's"), your figure is next to meaningless. Salaries are almost always negotiable—to your advantage. This negotiation should take place during the final interview.

Remember that "salary" isn't simply one number. It's a combination of benefits: insurance, pension plans, expense accounts, vacation and leave time, stock options and profit-sharing, free memberships and tuitions, free or low-cost day care, to name some. In a good company, these "fringes" may be quite substantial. But you won't know about them until the interview stage.

- ### Don't say why you want to leave your present job.

This is another matter for the interview. Reasons for making a job move are often complex: low pay, lack of opportunity, poor working conditions, a difficult boss, boredom, etc. The trouble is, those reasons are usually negative; they'll make you look bad. Employers want men and women who can function competently and creatively in spite of difficulties.

- **Don't draw attention to your lack of experience or to areas of professional weakness.**

Don't Do This

"I have had no work experience except during summer vacations and Christmas holidays."

Do This

"As a Little League coach for three summers, I learned organizational and managerial skills, effective teaching strategies, and public relations (especially during a losing season!)."

Don't Do This

"While I've never had any direct experience in advertising, I think I have the appropriate skills."

Do This

"With a B.A. in communications, good office skills, sales experience, and a strong interest in advertising, I think I'm a good candidate for your advertising trainee position."

Answering a Newspaper Advertisement

There are two advantages to responding to the classified ads in the newspaper. First, there is a definite opening and the organization wants it filled quickly. Second, the ad lists a specific job title, requirements, and sometimes responsibilities, so you can tailor your letter to the organization's needs.

That's the good news. The bad news is that most career professionals say that answering ads is the least effective way to get a job. They feel there is just too much competition. However, it *has* worked for some people. Here are some ways to make it work for you.

Note the requirements and analyze how closely you can come to meeting them. But note: You don't have to fill the requirements perfectly to apply for the job—or to get it. Don't count yourself out if you've had three years' experience and the ad says "five," or if you type 45 wpm and the ad says 60 wpm are necessary. If you're a strong enough candidate, you still stand a chance of getting the job.

Instead of trying for a perfect match between yourself and the job requirements, stress the skills you've got.

If an ad says that "five years' experience" is required, the organization is signaling a need for professionalism, strong skills, a thorough knowledge of the field, and the ability to do the job quickly with a cool head. In other words, designating a specific length of employment is shorthand for a whole lot of other qualities. Do you have those qualities (if not the years)? Say so.

If you can do so within the bounds of good taste and professionalism, make your letter unique in some way so that it will stand out from its competitors. Try a strong opening—for example, an attention-getting fact or even a good-natured "hello." Write the letter in memo fashion. Make a bulleted list of your skills. Describe (concisely) the two or three most significant accomplishments of your work life.

You don't have to mention salary or fee expectations if you don't want to. Asking for salary requirements is a technique advertisers use to get the best person at the lowest bid. You may simply ignore salary, or suggest a (wide) range (e.g., $20,000–25,000), adding a phrase like "depending on responsibilities and benefits." (Remember, salary is almost always negotiable.)

Don't write to the advertiser: "Please consider my application for the position of financial analyst as advertised in this Sunday's *Times.*" You can't really apply for a job with a company you know very little about. Your application is contingent on talking to that company and finding out who and what it is. In the letter, simply present yourself attractively and say that you'll look forward to meeting.

If the ad is a blind ad—that is, with no company name or telephone number given, only a box number—then of course you can't do the telephoning. Therefore, you must strongly suggest an action—that you be called for interview. At the end of letter, list your phone number (even if it's given elsewhere) and give convenient times when you may be reached. This ends the letter on a note of positive expectation; you're confident they'll give you a call.

> "My work phone is 777-4343. You can reach me there every weekday between 10 and 6. I look forward to hearing from you."

Even if the ad asks for a resume, you don't have to send one. You may write a "pitch" letter instead.

The "Pitch" Letter

Not every job application letter needs to "cover" a resume. Perhaps your work history isn't long or strong enough to produce an effective resume, but you have gained skills in volunteer, part-time, temporary, or at-home work. Or perhaps your resume may have something to cause it to be screened out (lack of specific requirements, for example). *You don't have to send a resume.*

Instead, write a one- or two-page letter, pitching yourself to the prospective employer. Focus this letter on that aspect of your work history that's relevant to the job you want. Following the directions for writing strong cover letters, be concise, specific, and hit on your accomplishments and skills.

In this letter, don't draw attention to the absent resume. Simply bring it along with you to the interview.

Saying Thank-You

Following all personal contacts with prospective employers—information or job interviews—sit down promptly and write a brief thank-you. It's simple courtesy and it shows you appreciate the courtesy which was extended to you.

Furthermore, writing thanks to each person you talk to may be a crucial element in landing a job. According to Richard Bolles, one survey cites this thank-you note as the most significant factor in the entire job-hunting process. It's worth the small effort, therefore.

And the thank-you letter may be the most pleasant piece of writing you do during your job hunt. Unlike most query and cover letters, this one is based on personal contact. You've met the person you're writing to, and you've shared some time and thought. You're able, therefore, to match the tone of your letter with the style and interests of the person. If the employer was open, friendly, and generally informal, your letter can be informal too (if that's what *you* feel comfortable with). If the employer was reserved or conservative, then your letter should be consistent with that formality.

In addition to showing that you have good social skills, the thank-you letter has other important functions. In it, you can:

• **Provide an immediate reminder of your meeting.**

Coming only a few days after your meeting, your letter gives positive reinforcement to it. It brings back your presence, the discussion, and your resume. This is an effective piece of public relations for you.

• **Emphasize your understanding of things.**

You can clarify what was discussed by putting it in writing—the company's goals, its hiring procedures, possible salary range, etc. This gives you a chance to clear up possible misunderstandings as well as to show you were listening. And sometimes, it's wise to remind an employer that he made a commitment, a promise, or a suggestion.

> "I'm glad you think that the personnel director should have broadened duties, especially in the areas of job discrimination and in-house mobility."

> "I want you to know that I liked everything about Serenity Publications and that I'm strongly interested in the position of Assistant Editor at a salary of $14,500."

> "I'll look forward to talking with you again after you've completed the move to your new offices. I'll give you a call on or about September 1, as you suggested."

- ## Reemphasize your skills, abilities, interests, and ideas.

> "I'm very interested in your long-range planning division. It's just the sort of process I've been involved with here at Otway. As I said yesterday, the best way to develop goals is to figure out ways to implement them."

- ## Pay a compliment to the company.

A thank-you letter gives you the opportunity to praise an organization in a justified, concrete way. You were there; you got a glimpse of its workings.

Praise is a delicate matter, however. Successful companies know they're successful; wide-eyed compliments may seem naive. The best strategy is to narrow the focus of your remarks. And of course, your admiration should be genuine.

> "Thank you for showing me the computer system. It is definitely state-of-the-art, but what impressed me most was your down-to-earth uses of it. I especially liked the idea of leasing the computers at off-hours to employees for personal use."

- ## Show you took some action.

If you've taken some action suggested during the interview—for example, made a contact—then say so. It will show you to be someone who listens well, takes advantage of help offered, and is good at follow-up.

> "I called Bill Thomas, and I'm going to meet him next Monday and see the plant. He was, as you said he'd be, friendly and helpful. Thanks for suggesting his name to me."

> "I located that article in *Business Week* you mentioned. Thanks—it was useful. It gave me all the facts and figures I needed in a convenient form."

- ## "Rewrite" the interview itself.

In the thank-you letter, you can add something you forgot to mention, revise something you said, or correct a misunderstanding.

Do this lightly, however. Don't sound as if you've made a serious mistake or that the interview was anything but successful. Keep your language positive, not negative.

Don't Do This

"I didn't mean to leave the impression that I'm really a Yale graduate. I departed from Yale after two years to go to Ohio State."

Do This

"I took my degree at Ohio State, by the way, not Yale. But I have very happy memories of my two years in New Haven."

Don't Do This

"I sure goofed yesterday when I told you that Otway Products grosses three million dollars a year—it's thirty million dollars."

Do This

"By the way, I mentioned yesterday that Otway Products has a yearly gross income of three million dollars. Of course, the figure is thirty million dollars."

Quitting a Job

When you decide to leave your job, you'll give your boss a formal resignation letter, probably following a face-to-face talk. A copy of this letter, addressed to your boss, will end up in the personnel files. It is an important letter because it documents your reasons for quitting and puts on paper the facts of your new job.

There is only one public reason to give for quitting, and that is that you've been offered a better opportunity. The real reason may be lousy pay or an intolerable boss at your present job. Never mind. That doesn't go into your resignation letter. Do not burn your bridges in print. Exit gracefully.

If you've liked your work and can say good things about it, do so. Praise the kindness of colleagues, the helpfulness of higher-ups: "Thanks again for your encouragement and help." Mention a new product, procedure, or project: "I look forward to hearing about the success of the Whitmore account." If nothing else, you can probably say with honesty that the experience was educational: "I've learned a great deal during my four years here."

While you're graciously complimenting your old company, make sure you put in a strong word for your new job. "I have accepted the position of Director of Personnel at American Widget where my first duties will be to design a new training and development program and write job descriptions for 50 new positions in marketing." You don't have to bring out a brass band here; a few specifics are enough. But if, in a few years, someone has forgotten where you went, this letter tells them: You're the one that got that great job at American Widget.

Typing the Letter

Appearance

- Use unmarked white or off-white paper, 8½ × 11 inches.
- *Or* use private business stationery if you're in business for yourself. It's not good form to use the letterhead of the company you're leaving. (This doesn't apply if you're a college teacher.)
- Do not use personalized or monogrammed stationery, or stationery with decorative flourishes like flowers or expressions like "Nancy's Notes" or "From the desk of. . . ."
- Type your letter. Handwriting is not acceptable.
- Use black ink. Don't use colored ribbons. Clean your typewriter keys.
- Restrict the letter to one page. If you have a second page, use a plain sheet of paper, not letterhead. Don't type on the back of the first sheet.

Matters of Form

- In the salutation, you may address your correspondent with her full name. In this way, you avoid the choices of Miss, Mrs., or Ms. The safest title is Ms., but you should know that some conservative institutions (e.g., *The New York Times*) don't use it. Persons with formal titles are addressed Dr., Dean, Professor, and so forth.
- Salutations are followed with a colon. Commas are used to express informal relations with the correspondent.
- Any of these closing phrases is acceptable: Yours, Yours truly, Sincerely, Sincerely yours, Very truly yours, or Best wishes.
- Instead of adding the usual "enc." meaning you've enclosed additional material, why not add a postscript:

PS: Here's my resume.

Sample Letters

LETTER REQUESTING AN INFORMATION
INTERVIEW
(Sent Without a Resume)

451 Reddington Street
Chicago, Illinois 60652
(312) 555-9456
April 25, 19--

Claire O'Malley
President
O'Malley, Pears & Preston
1000 Riverside Towers
East Circle Avenue
Chicago, Illinois 60631

Dear Claire O'Malley:

I'm not looking for work at present. But I am thinking
about changing jobs -- specifically, to public relations.
Dave Wilson suggested I contact you. He said that you
could answer most of my questions -- and that if you
couldn't, you'd know who could.

I am an English teacher and principal of the Green Street
School, two jobs which require strong skills in
communications and public relations. In addition, I am
the publicity coordinator for our community theater, the
Cowardly Lion Players. I managed Joe Dalton's successful
campaign for city council last year, and I'm a regular
contributor of op-ed pieces to The Chicago Tribune and the
South Side Weekly News.

If I could see you briefly -- say, twenty minutes -- at
your convenience, I'd greatly appreciate it. I'll give you
a call after the weekend.

Sincerely yours,

R.R. Pinney

LETTER REQUESTING AN INFORMATION INTERVIEW
(Sent Without a Resume)

98 Florian Street
Wellfleet, Mass.   02130
(617) 555-3491
May 23, 19--

Doris Stubbs
Director
Office of Urban Planning
Boston, Mass.   02138

Dear Doris Stubbs:

I'm not looking for a job right now, but I'd
very much appreciate a chance to talk with you.

I'm a successful real estate broker and my work
has given me a working knowledge of a broad range of
subjects -- building and zoning restrictions, tax law,
utility rates, financing, and historical preservation.
I'm thinking of making a career change, and I think that
many of my skills could be turned to problem-solving in
an organization like yours.

I've been especially interested in the Office
of Urban Planning since I read in the Boston Globe of its
commitment to "neighborhood integrity" as well as to
finding solutions to the middle-income housing shortage.

I'll give you a call next week to see when we
might meet at your convenience.

Very truly yours,

Robert French

A COVER LETTER
(Sent With a Resume)

777 Church Street
Memphis, Tennessee 38103
(901) 555-2627
December 4, 19--

Frank Dobson .
Vice-President of Personnel
Happy Hills Hotel Corporation
Two Hills Plaza
Memphis, Tennessee 38103

Dear Frank Dobson:

Could you use a person with strong administrative skills
in the area of human resources?

Here are some of my accomplishments as an Administrative
Aide in the Police Department:

I assisted my boss in holding a series of discussions
explaining revised procedures to one of our special
units and initiated a follow-up procedure for officers.
The discussions and follow-ups have proved so successful
that they are being used in other divisions.

I researched and compiled a resource manual of job
functions. To do this, I worked closely with dozens of
men and women in my department, learned to listen
carefully, and communicated what I learned in concise
written form.

As shop steward of Local 88 of AFSCME, I acted as
liaison between union and office workers, providing
information and interpreting forms to more than
200 employees.

May I talk to you about my ideas for communicating
company policy to employees, developing employee
potential through trainee programs and continuing
education, and streamlining recruiting methods?

I hope you don't mind if I call on Monday to set up
a convenient time to meet.

Yours,

Edwina Houck

P.S. Here's my resume.

Excerpts From Cover Letters

I like what I've read and heard about your company--
especially its interest in direct feedback from workers. I
like that because I'm a great believer in listening to people.
This simple strategy often solves a lot of problems.

I think my listening skills may be one of the reasons
that productivity is up 23 percent in the division I head at
a time when productivity is down in other departments.

Of course, my organizational skills are first-rate;
that's why my clients love me. But they also tell me that
when deadlines draw near and pressures mount, they can
count on my general good nature and unflappability. I
enjoy being the calm at the eye of the storm.

Couldn't you use this combination of productivity
and cool?

Winning makes me happy. I'm very happy right now
because, as marketing manager for my company's northwest
division, responsible for 15 yearly campaigns, I've been
increasing sales by an average of 40 percent every year for
the past four years.

I've been watching the Geist Company's commitment
to growth for some time now, starting back in 1979
when the Examiner praised you as "the Cinderella company."
When Jerry Breuer told me you have an opening for a national
marketing director, I thought I'd contact you.

I love my work and I like my company, but I'd like
a chance to talk to you about the position. And I'd like
to share with you some of my ideas for innovative campaigns

and for improving communications with field representatives.

I'll call next Tuesday to set up a convenient time to meet.

My summer job in the congressman's office required strong office skills: fast, accurate typing and informal shorthand. In addition, it improved my writing skills -- I researched and wrote the answers to hundreds of pieces of constituent mail. But, perhaps most importantly, I got a practical, grass-roots perspective on local and national politics.

My degree in engineering isn't enough. As the first woman production supervisor here at ChemCo, I've discovered that people skills are just as important as engineering skills. I'm proud that my all-male crew of 20 machinists and mechanics won both the plant Safety Award and Quality Control Award last year.

You may be interested in some of the other things I've done:

  --Designed new and more efficient equipment for
    our new plant.

  --Revised outdated report forms.

  --Coordinated monthly meetings with the company
    president and plant supervisors to discuss
    improved productivity and better safety.

  --Represented my company at the Annual Plant Safety
    Conference in Cleveland this year.

THE "PITCH" LETTER
(Sent Without a Resume)

2055 Sylvosa Street
Phoenix, Arizona 85022
August 2, 19--

John L. Hall
Director, Office of Development
St. Cecilia's Hospital
One Sahuaro Plaza
Phoenix, Arizona 85020

Dear John Hall:

I read with great interest last week's article in the Gazette in which you said, "Our institutional grants have increased, but I'm still hoping to increase community awareness and support of our services."

I have some strong skills which could help you reach that goal -- skills which I developed as 1982 program coordinator of the Heart Fund. Some of my specific accomplishments are:

- I raised $200,000 -- the most successful campaign in the Fund's history.

- I wrote weekly press releases and improved press contact so that coverage was increased 50 percent over the previous year.

- I produced a series of public service announcements for radio called "Heart Line."

- I reduced office expenses by 10 percent by streamlining accounting procedures.

I have some ideas which I'd like to share with you about getting improved local and national coverage of St. Cecelia's hospice, community outreach, alcoholism, and home care for the elderly programs.

May we discuss these issues at a time convenient to you? I'll give you a call on Wednesday.

Sincerely,

Jennifer Parks

LETTER RESPONDING TO A NEWSPAPER AD
(With Resume)

The Ad:

> ### ADMINISTRATIVE
> ### ASSISTANT
> Vice-President, Operations, seeks experienced admin. asst. Position requires excellent typing & steno, good comm. skills, ability to work w/people, and proven record of dependability.

The
Letter:

88 Heights Road
Cranbury, N.J.   08512
October 2, 19--

T1000
The New York Times
New York, N.Y.   10108

Dear New York Times Advertiser:

Good morning!

Office skills:
Typing -- 70 wpm
Steno -- 90 wpm
Experience on word processor -- Wang and Vydec

People skills:
I enjoy working with people.
I have a good telephone manner.

Communication skills:
I possess good writing and spelling skills.
My boss counts on me to prepare correspondence on my own.

Organizational skills:
I give my boss a daily folder filled with the correspondence,
    memos, research materials, biographical and financial
    information she needs for that day's meetings and events.
With my boss, I rewrote our department's annual budget.
I revised inventory procedures to keep supplies current.

Dependability:
I've been with my present company for four years, promoted
    steadily from receptionist to my present position of
    Executive Secretary.

My telephone number is (609) 555-6376. I look forward
to hearing from you.

Yours sincerely,

A THANK-YOU LETTER

110 Etra Road
Cranbury, New Jersey 08512
(609) 555-0412
October 2, 19--

R. Phillip Avery
President
The Delight Toy Corporation
One World Trade Center
New York, New York 10047

Dear Phillip Avery:

Thank you for seeing me yesterday. It was a great
help to hear first-hand about the Delight Toy Corporation.
I appreciate the time you took to meet with me.

I was especially interested in hearing about the
marketing plans for your new Do-and-Learn products.
It's a well-designed line and looks like it can take
a big bite out of the competition. I agree with you --
coordination between the national advertising campaign
and store layout and merchandise presentation is crucial.

I'm very interested in the position of manager
of your new Glassboro branch. I believe my experience
at Kid's Stuff Clothes has given me strong skills in
office and business management, financial planning,
personnel selection, and store organization -- skills
which make me a strong candidate to join your winning team.

I look forward to hearing from you. And again,
thanks very much for talking with me.

Best wishes,

Tom Bucknell

Bibliography for Job Hunters

Basic Reference Works

Dictionary of Occupational Titles. U.S. Department of Labor. Latest edition.

Occupational Outlook Handbook. U.S. Department of Labor. Latest edition.

Renetzky, Alvin (ed.). *Directory of Career Training and Development Programs*. Ready Reference Press, 1979.

Books

Bolles, Richard Nelson. *What Color is Your Parachute?* Ten Speed Press. New edition every year.

Chastain, Sherry. *Winning the Salary Game: Salary Negotiation for Women*. John Wiley and Sons, Inc., 1980.

Figler, Howard. *The Complete Job-Search Handbook*. Holt, Rinehart & Winston, 1979.

Jackson, Tom. *Hidden Job Market*. Times Books, 1976.

Jackson, Tom. *28 Days to a Better Job*. Hawthorn Books, Inc., 1977.

Lathrop, Richard. *Who's Hiring Who*. Ten Speed Press, 1977.

Scheele, Adele. *Skills for Success*. Ballantine Books, Inc., 1979.

What to Do with The Rest of Your Life. Staff of Catalyst. Simon & Schuster, 1980.

Magazines

(Ask the librarian for special-interest magazines such as *Health Careers Digest*.)

Ad Search
Career World
Chronicle of Higher Education
Jobs in Print
Wall Street Journal National Business Employment Weekly
Working Woman (Highly recommended for both men and women; especially strong on techniques for job hunting in government).

8.

ABC'S OF USAGE

Abbreviations

In formal writing or business writing, the general practice is to spell out most words, except those commonly abbreviated like Dr., Mrs., a.m., B.C., rpm, mph, St. (for Saint).

- **Spell out the names of places.**

  United States
  Soviet Union (not U.S.S.R.)
  Coffee County

- **Spell out words like Street, Avenue, Building, Square.**

  Fifth Avenue at lunch hour is a fashion show.
  She wanted to go to Hampton Court.

- **Spell out months and days.**

  February
  Tuesday

The names of well-known organizations and government agencies are not usually spelled out and periods are left out of the abbreviations.

FTC	CBS	AFL–CIO
CIA	YWCA	AT&T
UN	YMHA	IBM

It will depend on your audience whether you need to spell out, for the first usage, such names as the American Federation of Television & Radio Artists (AFTRA) or The National Institutes of Health (NIH).

For abbreviations of parts of names such as Limited, Company, Incorporated, and *and,* check the firm's own spelling.

> Harper & Row, Publishers, Inc.
> Xerox Corporation
> Babson Mfg. Co., Inc.
> Targer & Daughters, Ltd.

Adjectives and Adverbs

Adjectives make nouns more specific. We can speak of not just any bicycle, but a *new, red* bicycle. Adverbs do the same thing for verbs. I ran not just any way, but *slowly* and *breathlessly.*

Adjectives and adverbs are modifiers. Modify comes from a Latin word meaning to limit; they limit and restrict the meaning of other words. By calling the bicycle *new* and *red,* we can distinguish it from all the other bicycles in the bicycle stand.

The chief function of these modifiers is to give more information, to make writing clearer. They are often crucial to the writer's meaning.

Too many modifiers look like overwriting in business letters. They weaken the information being conveyed and they clutter up the page. The most common error is too many adverbs (or adverb phrases). The way to correct this is to substitute one strong verb for the verb-plus-verb phrase.

Not This	But This
I attempted with success	I succeeded
I spoke persuasively	I persuaded
I moved decisively	I decided
I assembled in an organized fashion	I organized

Affect/Effect

As verbs, these two words are often confused. They come from the same Latin root, *facere,* meaning to do or to make. Affect is formed with the prefix *a-,* which means *to;* it means to change or influence. Effect is formed with the prefix *e-,* which means *out;* it means to bring about or cause to happen.

> Her good spirits affected her whole family.
> The changes were effected by improved productivity.

As a noun, effect means result or influence.

> The effect of the air pollution was immediate.

All Together/ Altogether

All together means acting, being, or gathered in a group.

> Jimmy arrived at last, and the family was all together.

Altogether means wholly, entirely, or completely.

> This case is altogether different.

All Ready/ Already

All ready means everything is ready, all is prepared.

> The dinner is all ready by six o'clock.

Already means by this time or previously

> The dinner was already prepared when I arrived.

All Right/ Alright

All right means adequate or satisfactory. *Alright* is a common misspelling, which is gaining acceptance because of its popularity as a variant spelling. Use *all right* in formal writing.

Among/ Between

We must choose *among* three or more items. We must choose *between* two items.

And

It is acceptable to begin a sentence with *and;* in fact, it's a good transition word.

I began by taking an inventory of my professional assets. And I found, to my surprise, that I had some pretty good skills.

As Wilson Follett reminds us in *Modern American Usage:* "A prejudice lingers from the days of schoolmarmish rhetoric that a sentence should not begin with *and.* The supposed rule is without foundation in grammar, logic, or art."

And/ Or

And/or is legal language meaning this or that or both. But it is often unnecessary.

We could go for a ride and/or read a book.
We could go for a ride or read a book.

Capitalization

- **Capitalize the proper names of people, places, buildings, and things, and words that are an essential part of proper names.**

> Princeton Junction, New Jersey
> Brooklyn Bridge
> Niagara Falls
> Dodge Dart
> St. Marks Church
> Bronx Zoo
> Palace Theatre
> The Cincinnati Kid
> Old West

- **Capitalize names of institutions and organizations.**

> Department of Defense
> Job Placement Bureau
> Boston Red Sox

- **Capitalize titles before a name or titles of high rank appearing alone.**

> Mayor Cohen
> the President of the United States
> Dr. English
> Bishop Ginger

- **Do NOT capitalize titles appearing alone.**

> The mayor of our town is Marvin Cohen.
> The president of the company is coming today.
> Has anyone seen the doctor?

- **Do NOT capitalize places and buildings not appearing as a part of a proper name.**

> The zoo is in the Bronx.
> The doctor's name is English.

- **Do NOT capitalize names of centuries or decades.**

> the eighteenth century
> the roaring twenties
> the fifties

- **You *may* capitalize regions of the country: the South, the Northeast. But do NOT capitalize directions.**

> I was a child of the American West.
> The birds flew south.

Capitalize south, north, etc., when they are part of a name, a place, or an address.

> You can be guided by the North Star.
> She lived at 100 East Lexington for years.
> His address, of course, is 1776 Pennsylvania Avenue, SW.

Cliches

Cliches are trite expressions which were once fresh but have become stale through overuse. For example, we say "busy as a bee" without thinking about the originally fresh image of a bee, ceaselessly buzzing from flower to flower. We speak of something coming "out of the blue," without thinking of the force of a materialization in the blue sky.

Euphemisms are less direct, less offensive substitutes for other words or phrases; they are almost always cliches. "Passed on" is a euphemism for "died," for example. Sometimes euphemisms are called for, but, in general, they are better avoided. "Passed on" does not change the fact of death and may even diminish its significance. (You won't find "passed on" in most sacred religious texts.) Another example is "senior citizen" for an old person.

Jargon is the "in" language of specialized populations—computer programmers, doctors, businesspeople, teachers, etc. Almost every group of people has a special language and knowing it is a sign of belonging to the tribe. When jargon hits the general population it turns into a cliche pretty fast. Some current jargon words are *concept* (for *idea* or *plan*), *viable* (for *workable* or *practical*), *upgrade* (for *improve*), *entity* (for *thing* or *organization*), and *system* (as in "skin care system"; omit).

My least favorite cliche is this one:

Today's contemporary society

The first two words repeat themselves; in fact, neither one is necessary since we assume "our society" to be the current one. This phrase often turns up in a larger cliche, usually looking something like this: "In the hustle and bustle of today's contemporary society." It's a cliche deeply rooted in our view of ourselves; things are different now, we think. There's the Bomb, and the telephone; cold war and detente; the Middle East and whatever it is that goes on in California; cancer and urban blight; divorce and unemployment. But many other societies have had equally dark stresses. It helps to remember that Shakespeare's London, for example, was also a place of "hustle and bustle." There was a great deal of street crime; the Thames was polluted; the plague killed off hundreds; the court system wasn't just and execution was by public hanging (heads of decapitated criminals adorned London Bridge); the food wasn't good and people smoked too much (King James wrote a pamphlet suggesting cutting down).

Examine the validity of the cliches you use. Try to write without them. Even if you cannot be original, you can at least speak clearly and directly, without using the smokescreen of the overworked expression.

Council/ Counsel/ Consul

Council is a legislative body or an association of people or organizations.

He belongs to the Council on Foreign Relations.

Counsel is advice or recommendation. It also means a lawyer or a group of lawyers.

> She could give him good counsel.
> Please talk to my counsel about that matter.

Consul is a kind of ambassador to a foreign country.

> He is our country's consul in Mauritania.

Danglers

Danglers are phrases which float in a sentence; the phrase doesn't clearly refer to another word in the sentence. Writers most commonly put danglers at the beginning of a sentence.

Dangling: While backing down the driveway, the car suddenly hit mud and ice.
Revised: While I was backing down the driveway, the car suddenly hit mud and ice.

Dangling: Well-educated and stunningly tall, her books are pure Gothic.
Revised: She is well-educated and stunningly tall. Her books are pure Gothic.

Dangling: Singing in the rain, my sandals fell off.
Revised: My sandals fell off while I was singing in the rain.

Exclamation Point

Use sparingly.

Hopefully

This word is an adverb, meaning "with hope." It is correctly used in the following sentence.

Waiting for an answer, she looked at him hopefully.

Hopefully is widely misused, probably because it is useful to express the idea "it is hoped" or "I hope." It is incorrectly used in the following sentence.

Hopefully, the pitcher will strike him out.

Presumably, the pitcher isn't pitching with hope but with a speedball or a slider. You can see that "hopefully" merely dangles in this sentence and doesn't specifically modify any part of the sentence.

As a dangler, *hopefully* continues to turn up in the speech of well-educated people and may someday gain acceptance in writing. But, as of now, this usage is still unacceptable.

Finalize

-Ize is a suffix which forms words like burglarize or Americanize. But recent usage has tacked *-ize* onto nouns with reckless abandon to form a number of non-words, or jargon words. For *finalize*, write *make final;* for *prioritize*, write *put in order;* for *utilize*, write *use. Personalize* is often unnecessary.

I.e./ E.g.

I.e. stands for the Latin phrase *id est*, that is. It is used to amplify a statement, or introduce an explanation or definition.

The carrots were cut in a matchstick julienne, i.e., in a dice about the size and length of matchsticks.

E.g. stands for the Latin phrase *exempli gratia,* for example.

I've taught many freshman courses—e.g., composition, rhetoric, and speech.

In business letters it's often smoother and more readable to write "that is to say" for i.e. and "for example" for e.g.

I've taught many freshman courses—for example, composition, rhetoric, and speech.

Imply/ Infer

Writers imply; readers infer. *Imply* means to suggest or to indicate without saying openly or directly. *Infer* means to draw a conclusion or derive by reasoning.

She implied in her statement that the Dean was responsible.
I inferred from her statement that the Dean was responsible.

Literally

Literally means actually or really. It is used correctly here.

I was literally in deep water; my house was flooded.

But it is often misused as an intensifier, and is used to mean the opposite of literal truth.

He was literally sending up smoke signals to get attention at the meeting.

- Me/ I

Me is used as the object of a preposition or a verb; *I* is used as the subject of a sentence. Don't use *I* incorrectly as the object in order to sound refined.

Incorrect

There is no one better read than I.
Won't you join my husband and I?

Correct

There is no one better read than me.
Won't you join my husband and me?

Numbers

- **Spell out numbers one to ninety-nine.**

- **Spell out numbers that begin a sentence.**
  Two hundred years was quite enough.

- **Spell out numbers that are in the millions and billions.**
  The annual book budget is forty-three million dollars.

- **Use figures for all other numbers.**
  There are 5,467 residents of Blue, Oklahoma.

Prepositions at End of Sentence

It is acceptable to end a sentence with a preposition. Trying to avoid this often produces awkward sentences.

Awkward

Can you tell me the name of the building in which I will be staying?

That's the area on which I have obtained the most information.

Revised

Can you tell me the name of the building I will be staying in?

That's the area I have obtained the most information on.

Plurals

- **Most plurals are formed by adding *s* to the noun.**

  apple, apples   paper, papers   house, houses

- **Nouns ending in *s, x, z, ch,* or *sh* often form the plural by adding *es*.**

  process, processes   tax, taxes   birch, birches

- **Add *s* for nouns ending in a vowel plus *o* or *y*.**

  radio, radios   boy, boys

- **Add *es* for nouns ending in a consonant and *o*.**

  hero, heroes

- **For nouns ending in a consonant plus *y*, form the plural by changing the *y* to *i* and adding *es*.**

  ferry, ferries   candy, candies

- **Form the plural of proper names by *s* or *es*.**

    Hall, Halls   French, Frenches   Jones, Joneses

- **Add an *s* to form the plural of numbers, dates, or capital letters.**

    the 1880s   As and Bs   three 7s

- **Add *s* or change *y* to *i* and add *es* to form plurals of numbers written out.**

    several fours   three twenties

- **Add an apostrophe plus *s* to avoid confusion.**

    A's   U's

- **Add an apostrophe and an *s* to form plurals of lower-case letters and abbreviations.**

    Cross your t's and dot your i's.
    The P.O.W.'s have returned.

- **When a compound noun contains two or more words, form the plural by adding an *s* to the most important word.**

    attorneys-at-law
    mothers-in-law
    editors-in-chief
    lieutenant governors

Here is a list of nouns whose plural forms can cause confusion.

    spoonful, spoonfuls
    valley, valleys
    wife, wives
    species (singular and plural)
    series (singular and plural)
    fish (singular and plural)
    alumna, alumnae (female)
    alumnus, alumni (male)

datum, data
formula, formulas, formulae
index, indexes, indices
memorandum, memorandums, memoranda
memo, memos
criterion, criterions, criteria

Quotation Marks

Quotation marks are used when a person or other source is quoted directly.

John F. Kennedy said, "Ask not what your country can do for you; ask what you can do for your country."

Emerson writes of cattle that "seem to have great and tranquil thoughts."

In Dante's Hell, these words welcome the new inhabitant: "Abandon hope, all you who enter here."

But when the reference isn't quoted directly, then quotation marks aren't used.

Kennedy reminded us to ask what we can do for our country.

Quotation marks are often misused to set aside slang expressions or expressions that are not part of standard English. Quotation marks used like this are at once apologetic and attention-getting; they are overly cute. Either omit the marks or omit the phrase you are apologizing for.

Not: The new budget leaves us "sitting pretty."
But: The new budget leaves us sitting pretty.
The new budget leaves us in good shape.

Spelling

Spelling, like all other components of usage, tends to get simplified. One of my favorite Americanisms is the name of a self-service gas station, deep in the hills of Alabama, where I once stopped. The name was spelled just as the local population must have pronounced it: Hep-U-Sef.

But in business writing you should avoid streamlined spellings: nite, thru, wash'n'dry, donut. Some standard expressions are acceptable, however: rock 'n' roll, for example.

Here is a list of correct spellings for commonly misspelled words.

absence	maintenance
abundance	mathematics
accommodate	misspelling
achievement	necessary
acquire	occasion
all right	occurred
arguing	parallel
apparatus	particular
beginning	personal
category	personnel
comparative	Pittsburgh
competent	possession
conscious	practical
definitely	precede (come before)
develop	proceed (advance)
discernible	prejudice
effect	principal
embarrass	privilege
fascinate	psychology
fulfill	recommend
grievance	referring
height	reminisce
hypocrisy	roommate
its (possessive pronoun)	rhythm
it's (it is)	seize
inadvertent	sense
incidentally	separate
indispensable	supersede
irresistible	their (possessive pronoun)
liaison	there

they're (they are)
theories
to
too
two
transferred
Tucson
unnecessary
undoubtedly
unusually
using
vacuum

vengeance
warrant
weather
whether
weird
writing
written
who's (who is)
whose (possessive pronoun)
yield
your
you're (you are)

Index